CULTURAL ADAPTATION
OF THE LITURGY

Anscar J. Chupungco, O.S.B.

CULTURAL ADAPTATION
of
THE LITURGY

PAULIST PRESS ◆ *New York/Ramsey*

Library of Congress
Catalog Card Number: 82-80161

ISBN: 0-8091-2452-1

Published by *Paulist Press*
545 Island Road, Ramsey, N.J. 07446

Printed and bound in the United States of America

Contents

Introduction

Many years of research and work of revision were spent to give the Roman liturgy the shape envisioned by Vatican II. Practically all the important liturgical books are now published, and some of them have been revised a second time in the light of the more recent needs of local churches and the latest findings of scholars. True to the spirit of Vatican II the Church continues to renew and reshape her liturgy, "in order that the Christian people may more securely derive an abundance of graces from the sacred liturgy" (SC 21). However, there is an aspect of liturgical renewal which needs an urgent and more careful attention. It is not enough to reshape every now and then the texts and rituals of the Roman liturgy according to the pastoral needs here and now and the dictates of liturgical scholarship. Renewal implies also the realization of those "links between the message of salvation and human culture," especially when the Church gives that message a better expression in liturgical celebrations (GS 58). Liturgical renewal has also to address itself to the question of liturgical adaptation to various cultures.

The cultural dimension of the liturgy is the focus of this book. The first chapter deals with the historical aspect of the question, while the second attempts to interpret the mind of Vatican II's SC 37–40 on adaptation. The third, fourth and fifth chapters discuss what the author proposes as basic principles of adaptation derived from theology, liturgy and culture. Many years of research, conversations with experts and active participation in projects of liturgical adaptation have gone into this book. In writing it the author has made use of his other publications on the subject, especially some pertinent sections of his book *Towards a Filipino Liturgy* (Manila, 1976). It is the author's hope that this work will provide material not only for information but also for stimulating attempts of adaptation in local churches.

Many people have contributed to the writing and publication of this book. Among them three deserve special mention for their encouragement and editorial and technical assistance: Professor Adrien Nocent, Prof. Moises Andrade and Prof. Wilton Gregory. To them and to all who have enriched this book by their comments and suggestions the author expresses deep appreciation.

I
A History of
Liturgical Adaptation

History offers a convincing argument in favor of liturgical adaptation. It assures the Church that adaptation to various cultures has been a constant feature of Christian liturgy. Indeed it is part and parcel of her tradition. The apostles did it, and so did the Fathers of the Church and her pastors far into the Middle Ages. Adaptation of the liturgy to various native genius and tradition is not a novelty but fidelity to tradition. Liturgical adaptation is as old as the Church, but it has been brought to the limelight in modern times because of Vatican II's renewed sense of pluralism within the Church and respect for people's cultures.[1]

But history does not only assure the Church that adaptation is part of her long tradition: it also offers models to be imitated and pitfalls to be avoided. History teaches her how to take risks with creativity and how to be prudent with novelty. It can be said that the liturgical reform envisaged by Vatican II has taken this historical perspective into account. The Constitution on Sacred Liturgy (SC 23) requires careful theological, historical and pastoral investigation of each part of the liturgy which is to be revised. If sound tradition is to be retained, while legitimate progress is encouraged, a knowledge of historical facts becomes imperative.

By and large, modern liturgical renewal is conditioned by historical data, and the program of adaptation can be realized only in the light of historical development of liturgical forms.

This means in effect that progress in the liturgy has to recognize the process of evolution, whereby original forms are elaborated and brought to fuller development in the course of history.[2] Obviously not every detail of evolution has been felicitous or praiseworthy. SC 21 openly admits this when it says that liturgical elements subject to change "not only may, but ought to be changed with the passage of time if they have suffered from the intrusion of anything out of harmony with the inner nature of the liturgy or have become unsuited to it." Encumbrances and intrusions which the liturgy has suffered in the past have muddled the original clarity of the Roman rite. The reform aims to correct this by a return to the classical form of the Roman liturgy which was characterized by its simplicity, brevity and sobriety. SC 34 returns to this classical form: "The rites should be distinguished by a noble simplicity: they should be short, clear, and unencumbered by useless repetitions; they should be within the people's powers of comprehension, and normally should not require much explanation." It is here that research on the pristine state of the liturgy can guarantee what is authentic and what is an aberration, what is an improvement and what is an encumbrance. It will be far too short-sighted, however, to content oneself with the original form or to return to the New Testament and utterly ignore what transpired between the apostolic period and Vatican II. Twenty centuries of experience in the field of adaptation have certainly much to offer to the Church of today. Not only divinely instituted forms but also cultural elements adopted by the Church in the course of history merit our attention and respect.

In retracing the steps of history, one has to begin with the premise of the Church's enduring fidelity to the essentials of Christian revelation. She has lived every historical age before the Lord, faithfully preaching the Word, baptizing those who believe and celebrating the memorial of his paschal mystery.[3] But being a human community, the Church is contingent on the circumstances of culture, history and development of theological reflection. In one generation she may carry out the command of the Lord in the simplicity and intimacy of a household celebration, without external manifestation of a public kind. In another, imbibing the political circumstances of her people, she may celebrate the mystery of faith in the splendor of a Constantinian basilica. Or in the playful fantasy of another age, she may adorn the same mystery with the gaiety of the baroque period. Every age is its own justification, and not one should be accused of infidelity. Often we are tempted to inveigh against the intransigence of the Tridentine reform, or mock the flamboyance of the baroque liturgy which disregarded active and intelligent participation, magnified the external and dwarfed the essential. But already we begin to hear criticism of the new liturgy as being too austere, anemic and cold.[4] One wonders for how long some local churches, especially in the third world, can resist the temptation of retouching the new liturgy with some colorful and dramatic elements.

Interpretation of Historical Data

In interpreting historical data it is necessary to place them in their concrete situation. It is then that one discovers the relativity of historical evolution. Except for the more essential elements of faith and liturgical tradition, one may not expect a great deal of coherence and consistency in the way forms developed. The prayer of the faithful and the ministry of the homily are classic examples of how sociological and theological factors exerted influence in the liturgy.[5] Even such basic elements as the epiclesis and the primacy of the Word did not always receive the same degree of attention.[6] Likewise, the movement from pluralism to uniformity (and vice versa) is a recurring phenomenon[7] in the history of the liturgy. All this tells us that in being guided by historical data, we cannot choose one specific detail from the past in order to resuscitate it in the present, regardless of the historical circumstances that led to its disappearance or of the pastoral needs of the present, which may not warrant its revival. That the Eucharist, for instance, was first celebrated in the context of a meal, and later of an *agape*, is not enough reason for celebrating it now with the accessories of a modern dinner! But neither should one exclude the possibility of adapting liturgical usages from the past, if they are in accord with the culture and need of the people and with contemporary theological reflection.

The study of history is useful for another reason. One can always refer back to the original forms for a more authentic interpretation of liturgical practices still extant but of little or no significance to modern man's faith or prayer life. The rite of commingling in the Roman Mass will be more meaningful if explained according to its historical background (a fragment of consecrated bread sent by the Pope to the parish churches of Rome as a sign of ecclesial communion) rather than according to its mystical symbolism (the resurrection of Christ).[8] When certain elements of the Roman Mass are interpreted without due reference to history, there is danger of imposing false symbolism to rites that were purely practical in nature. This is the case of the washing of hands, originally a purely hygienic practice in the Roman rite,[9] which is now interpreted as "desire for interior purification."[10] It was lack of historical perspective and exaggerated emphasis on the sacrificial aspect of the Mass that led Amalar of Metz to interpret rituals in the context of the Passion narrative.[11] Symbolism can no doubt enrich the liturgy, but it should be based on historical data.

History should not be treated, therefore, either from the angle of romantic historicism or as a fossilized past with no relevance to the present.[12] Likewise historical data will have to be subjected to critical evaluation, in order that the experience of the past centuries may be assessed. Thus the Church may continue to draw inspiration and guidance from them.

Adaptation in the Apostolic Period

It is natural to preface this survey with the observation that Christianity began as a religious movement within Judaism.[13] This explains why the Christian liturgy, rooted as it is in the Jewish liturgy,[14] will forever be linked to its origins. It also accounts for the attitude of the first disciples toward religious cult, an attitude which they inherited from the Master himself. One is sometimes perplexed by the seemingly contradictory attitude of Christ toward the Jewish cult. On the one hand, he showed himself a faithful Jew who frequented the temple, preached in the synagogue, celebrated the Passover and took part in ritual sacrifices, or at least sanctioned them. On the other hand, he denounced the legalism of the cult, declared himself Lord of the sabbath, and announced the destruction of the temple and the advent of the new form of worship in spirit and in truth. The explanation probably lies in his declaration that he did not come to abolish the law and the prophets, but to bring them to perfection. It was not a question of rupture, but of perfecting the religion of his fathers. This he realized by giving a new orientation to the Jewish rites, imbuing them with his own mystery. The Last Supper is a case of reinterpretation of the paschal meal: no longer a memorial of the exodus, but of his passing over from this world to the Father for the salvation of mankind. Paul's commentary on the institution is a faithful echo of the Master's original design (1 Cor. 11:26). The baptism practiced by John and the Qumran community was also adopted by Christ as a sign of participation in the life of the Trinity in whose name it is to be celebrated. Peter's words to the crowd at Pentecost show that the disciples were already conscious of the Christological dimension of the ritual (Acts 2:38).

Following the example of Christ, the apostles frequented the temple, prayed in the tradition of the Jewish people, observed the law and probably offered sacrifices.[15] Acts 20:16 speaks of Paul's decision "to pass wide of Ephesus so as to avoid spending time in Asia, since he was anxious to be in Jerusalem, if possible, for the day of Pentecost." Imbued, however, with the recent experience of the Christ-event, the disciples of Jesus progressively infused a new meaning into the Jewish cult, reading the Scripture in the light of the Christian mystery and proclaiming this as the fulfillment of God's promise to Israel. Peter's, Stephen's and Paul's addresses, as reported in Acts, all bear the stamp of the new perspective in which the young Church understood and proclaimed the Word of God to Israel.[16]

The Jerusalem community, being deeply rooted in Jewish traditions, did not abandon the observance of the law. But the Hellenistic communities did, under the influence of Paul, who saw the provisional character of the law, its preparatory role in the coming of Christ and its inability to justify (Rom. 1:8–11, 36). It was not merely a question of abating the rigor of the law for the Gentiles; it was rather a question of principle, as one can gather from the speech of Peter to the assembly at Jerusalem (Acts 15:7–11). He affirmed that "God made no distinction between them and us, since he purified their hearts by faith" and that "we are saved in the same way as they are: through the grace of the Lord Jesus." Circumcision and the observance of the law of Moses were therefore a useless burden on pagans, whom God—James further argued—also chose as a people for himself. The solution reached was not one of total breach of ties with Judaism, but a compromise inspired by the spirit of charity and of ecclesial communion with Judaeo-Christians.[17] But the core of the Jerusalem liturgy, centering on baptism, the breaking of bread and the reading of Scripture, was handed over to the Hellenistic world in its original state, pure and unadulterated by explicit compromise with paganism.[18] It was not until the fourth century that Christian liturgy welcomed, under certain conditions, what was good and noble in pagan religions.[19]

The first disciples inherited also the intransigence of the Jewish religion. Pagan cult and its mystery rites were to be despised, for they were the worship of false gods and of the devil himself. Christianity could not make concessions to them in anything that would be prejudicial to its integrity. Its point of entry was not religion but philosophy. Paul, who strolled around Athens admiring its sacred monuments and caught the interest of the Council of Areopagus by calling its attention to an altar dedicated to an unknown god, explained the new doctrine in the philosophy of the day and appealed to the writings of the sages (Acts 17:22–29). But idols and sacrificial feasts were another thing. "You cannot drink the cup of the Lord and the cup of demons," Paul warned the Christians at Corinth; "you cannot take your share at the table of the Lord and at the table of demons" (1 Cor. 10:21–22).

One can describe the apostolic Church as a convergence of three strong currents. The first was the pervasive movement to imbue the Jewish cult with the mystery of Christ.[20] The traditional form, especially the synagogue, was not rejected,[21] but centered on the person of Christ. This attitude of not destroying but of rectifying, ennobling and reorienting the traditions of the chosen people characterized early Christianity's approach to adaptation. The importance of such an attitude should not be missed. As an historical religion, Christianity cannot abstract itself from its sources. Although the apostles shook off the burden of Mosaic law and adopted the language of Hellenistic Christians,[22] they scrupulously guarded those traditions which constituted a vital link with the original revelation of God to his people Israel. The second current was activated by the spirit of openness to the new situation brought about by the conversion of pagans. If the Christian message was to be shared outside of the confines of Judaism, accommodations had to be made.[23] It was a major step, one to which the apostles did not easily accede, thoroughly steeped as they were in their traditions. It took divine intervention and a council of the apostles and elders for the early Church to surrender to the inevitable. But it set a guiding principle for later adaptations.[24] The third current was conditioned by a tenacious disdain of pagan religions. This current sprang from Israel's ardent zeal for monotheism in a polytheistic world.[25] As long as Christianity was still a movement within Judaism and as long as its members were recruited from pagans who attended the synagogues, the climate of hostility to pagan feasts and rituals persisted. But as soon as Christianity had to settle in a non-Jewish milieu, it had to adapt and transform whatever was good and noble in paganism.[26]

Adaptation in the Age of Persecutions

This period exhibits features which are characteristic of the apostolic Church. One is the conscious effort to remain within the Jewish liturgical tradition, although within a radically changed perspective. Another is the incessant battle against pagan religions. The link with Judaism can be seen in the prayers composed during this period, whether they were used in the liturgy or not.[27] Without entering here into details, one may repeat the conclusion reached by various authors that the prayer in *1 Clement* 59–61 and the blessings in the book of *Didaché* are thoroughly Jewish in form, although they focus on the "servant" of God, Jesus Christ.[28] In explaining the meaning of baptism, Tertullian employs Old Testament types, thus establishing continuity between the Old and New Testaments in Christian sacraments.[29] Likewise, the prayers in the *Apostolic Tradition* of Hippolytus of Rome abound in allusions to the Old Testament figures.[30] One can indeed affirm that appreciation of these early prayers presupposes a broad scriptural background. The liturgy was not for the uninitiated but for those who had heard and accepted the preaching of the Word.[31]

Not only prayers, but also the liturgical art of this period breathes biblical themes. Doura-Europos, the house for the liturgy in Mesopotamia, is adorned with paintings depicting Adam and Eve, David and Goliath, the paralytic, Peter being saved in the sea, and the Good Shepherd.[32] In the Roman cemeteries before the fourth century the favorite themes are Noah, Isaac, Jonas, the raising of Lazarus, the adoration of the magi, the multiplication of loaves, the heavenly banquet, the Good Shepherd, the boat, and the woman at prayer.[33] With these examples one can gain an insight into the value that the Church of this period attached to Scripture.[34] Adaptation meant instilling Christian worship with salvation history. It meant that the events narrated in Scripture were realized in the liturgy and that the mystery of Christ was present in it. Liturgical art was not primarily adornment nor catechetical expression of the faith of the community gathered for worship.

It was a reminder that the liturgical celebration was in the mainstream of salvation history.

It was during the age of persecutions that the apostolic practice of celebrating the breaking of bread in private homes was "institutionalized." Rich families offered their houses for the use of the *ekklesia,* the worshiping community. Because of their physical plan these houses lent themselves easily to the liturgical needs of the Church. The Roman *tablinium* where the *paterfamilias* presided, the *atrium* where members of the family assembled, the *triclinium* or dining room, and the *impluvium,* which was a large tank of water, were a perfect setup for the liturgy. With little adjustments, then, these houses were transformed into fitting centers for the activity of the Church.[35] They housed the worshiping community and were consequently called *domus ecclesiae.* Doura-Europos in Mesopotamia, a Hellenistic house built in 200 A.D. and converted into a *domus ecclesiae* in 232, is a classic example of these houses.[36] Rome could count as many as forty such houses, the more famous of which are those found under the churches of John and Paul, Cecilia, Clement and Pudentiana.[37] The *domus ecclesiae* left a deep impression on the Church, for they symbolized her nature as household of God.[38] Adopting the setting of the Roman house with its noblest traditions of family life, the Church was able to celebrate her liturgy in a personal and intimate ambit. The symbolism did not escape Ignatius of Antioch who described the Church as God's family gathered before the bishop who represented the Father and who presided over her in the company of presbyters representing the council of apostles, while deacons who represented the servant of God, Jesus Christ, waited on.[39] Although there is a striking similarity between the Roman family system and the *domus ecclesiae,* it can be affirmed that Roman *domus ecclesiae* maintained the basic setup of the Jewish synagogue.[40]

This period, as we have pointed out, is marked by a zeal to maintain the link with Scripture and with the finest traditions of the Jewish liturgy.[41] However, one begins to sense here an attitude of independence which gradually grew into antipathy and climaxed in scorching denunciation of the Jews and their practices.[42] The zenith of such tendency would be remarkable in the Constantinian period. The *Didaché,* for example, directed its Christian readers not to fast with the hypocrites (Judaeo-Christians?) on Monday and Tuesday, but on Wednesday and Friday. Likewise, instead of reciting the Jewish Benedictions, *Shemoneh 'Esreh,* three times daily with the hypocrites, the Christians were to pray the Lord's Prayer.[43] It should be noted, however, that it was not a question of abandoning Jewish customs altogether, but of adapting them to the situation of the Church. Fasting and prayer were not to be neglected, but they were to be imbued with the new spirit.

Another feature of this period is the Church's first attempt to express the apostolic tradition in the language and rituals of a pagan culture, the Greco-Roman culture. It was a novelty that became an enduring principle for succeeding centuries. Again and again the Church would look back to the Greco-Roman period whenever she entered into a similar situation. It was a missionary period, full of tension between fidelity to Jewish religious traditions and the assumption of pagan cultural expressions.[44] How wide could the Church open the door to pagan culture without danger to her faith and worship? What were her criteria for accepting some elements of the Greco-Roman culture and for rejecting others? The tension was never resolved; it was merely buried in her consciousness. Time and again it would surface, especially in the missions. The famous (or infamous) Chinese rites controversy between 1610 and 1742 typifies the Church's seemingly ambiguous stance in the face of paganism. Even Vatican II's benevolent attitude toward cultural and religious expressions among the "new Gentiles" has not totally eased the fears of many Churchmen.[45]

In dealing with modern civilization one can quite easily distinguish religious rituals from the purely social and political. Religious rituals can, of course, occasion social affairs and make their presence felt at political gatherings. But the dichotomy between them can be taken as a matter of fact. Such, however, was not the case with ancient civilizations, nor with

many of those in Asia, Africa and Latin America. The neat
distinction between the religious and the profane is artificial
when applied to them.[46] One cannot conceive of the Greco-
Roman culture without its myths, divinities and temples.[47]
Nor can one empty the Chinese civilization of its ancestral
rites.[48] The 1939 *Plane Compertum* of the Propaganda Fide did
precisely the impossible, when it declared the Chinese ancestral rites to have lost their religious significance. The secularism of Western religion, commented the *Documentation
catholique,* has dispersed the darkness of paganism and superstition.[49] In view of this, one hesitates to distinguish cultural
elements that are merely social, and without any religious
overtone, from elements that are exclusively for cultic purposes. And yet at least a mental distinction is necessary for
the sake of clarity. In fact the Church of the Greco-Roman period indulged in such a distinction of cultural elements, and
she never abandoned it.

It should be noted that the liturgical adaptation to the
Greco-Roman culture was not the fruit of previous theological
reflection.[50] Today we often start from the theological imperative of ecclesial incarnation. We can do this because we have
twenty centuries to reflect upon. In the beginning the Church
felt no such imperative. Her members were mostly Jews and
pagans who were sympathetic to Judaism. There was therefore no urgency to tackle the problem of incorporating pagan
culture to the liturgy. The preoccupation at that time was how
to preserve the Jewish heritage and at the same time maintain the newness of Christianity. A glance at the book of *Didaché,* written between 90 and 120 A.D., reveals this tension.
Prayer texts are deeply imbedded in Jewish tradition, but
they center on Christ. Jewish practices are not rejected, but
they take on a Christological orientation. The rite of baptism
is devoid of any non-Jewish influence, as described in the way
the Essenes must have practiced it, but it is celebrated in the
name of the Holy Trinity. There is no suggestion of rites like
anointing[51] and renunciation.

But this period was brief, and soon the Church was accepting members with no Jewish background. These were Gentiles

who grew up in the ambit of pagan rituals, idol worship and sacrifices. In the third century the Church began to learn the delicate art of "compromise."[52] Again it was not the result of some abstract theological reflection, but of a need to adjust to a new situation. If these new members had to grasp the faith more fully, this had to be explained in their language and illustrated with ceremonies with which they were familiar.

The writings of apologists like Justin Martyr and Tertullian are typical of the Church's attitude toward pagan cult at that time. It was one of total contempt for anything connected with idol worship. Pagan gods, rituals and temples were creations of the devil himself, and a Christian could have nothing to do with them. Such an attitude of intransigence was not original to Christianity, but was inherited from Judaism's staunch monotheism. It can also be explained in the light of the Church's missionary experience. It is not unusual that converts turn fanatic. Conversion to Christianity implies aversion to paganism. But one should exclude the case of the Maya of Central America who took to synthesizing the old and the new religions, and the Chinese who would not easily accept a foreign religion which rejected ancestral worship. In the former case one can ask of course whether there was real conversion or fear of the Christian sword; in the latter, one can ask whether it is possible or even necessary to attack the very foundation of a civilization. To turn to Christ meant to turn away from the old religion, and the old religion was synonymous to Satan and his works and pomps. To find in the new worship such elements as would remind them of the religion they had abandoned would have been revolting.

Another reason for this behavior was probably the persecution. To defend the young Church against the force of paganism, it was necessary to extol the superiority of the former and demonstrate the weakness and corruption of the latter. It is therefore not surprising to come across patristic writings which ridicule pagan cultic practices, especially when they resemble Christian ones. Justin Martyr, for instance, accuses the worshipers of Mithras of counterfeiting the Christian Eucharist in their initiation rite. Secret formulas are recited over bread and water, and these are offered to the initiates.[53] In his book on baptism Tertullian mocks the initiation rites of Isis and Mithras and the rituals of lustration. They are expensive but worthless, extravagant but empty. Christian baptism, on the other hand, is at once simple, without charge, yet efficacious.[54] Even a writer like Clement of Alexandria who conveniently served himself with the language of mystery rites did not hesitate to deride them for their falsehood and corruption.[55]

The question takes on a different perspective in the face of cultural elements which are not strictly connected with worship. To have a global view of the matter it would be ideal to examine every aspect of the Christian liturgy before the fourth century. However, the few examples that can be gathered from the rite of Christian initiation can throw enough light on the subject. Tertullian, for example, uses the word *eiuratio* to describe baptismal renunciation.[56] It is a legal term and signifies withdrawal from a contract of service or partnership. Upon entering into the service of Christ the candidate withdraws from the service of Satan, which he renounces with all the vigor of the law. Tertullian also speaks of baptismal profession or fidelity to Christ as *sacramenti testatio* or *signaculum fidei*.[57] Again these are technical terms which refer to the soldier's oath of allegiance to the Roman emperor. Another example comes from Tertullian's treatise on baptism. There he mentions the rite of anointing after the baptismal bath. The anointing must have been done with a generous amount of oil poured on the crown of the head and allowed to flow down the naked body of the neophyte. As Tertullian vividly describes it, *in nobis carnaliter currit unctio*.[58] What is the meaning of this rite? Tertullian traces its origin to the Old Testament practice of anointing priests on the crown of their heads, as Moses did to Aaron. He insinuates that baptism confers on a Christian what anointing in the Old Testament conferred on the Israelites: priesthood. Anointing is a fitting illustration of this effect of baptism. However, we know that the Greeks and Romans anointed their bodies for different motives like physical therapy, physical fitness and athletic purposes. Ambrose of Milan kept the priestly significance of post-baptismal anointing, but gave the pre-baptismal rite a more cultural tone: *unctus es quasi athleta Christi.*[59]

The *Apostolic Tradition* of Hippolytus of Rome offers a fascinating example. At his First Communion the neophyte receives not only the eucharistic species but also milk and honey. This, explains Hippolytus, is to signify "the fulfillment of the promise God made to the patriarchs, that he would give them a land flowing with milk and honey."[60] Having crossed the River Jordan through baptism, the neophyte now enters the promised land and tastes of its blessings. The rite is an eloquent portrayal of Christian passover; its biblical theme reinforces the imagery. But this type of drink is not unique to Christians. Pre-Christian Romans gave milk and honey to their newborn as a sign of welcome into the family and as a protection from evil spirits.[61] Is it not possible that Hippolytus was inspired by it, adapted it and gave it a biblical interpretation? The similarity is too striking to be dismissed as pure coincidence.

The contribution of culture is quite remarkable in the early stage of ritual development. But culture was not accepted into the liturgy without discrimination and reorientation. The Fathers always interpreted in the light of Christ what culture had to offer. *Eiuratio* means renunciation of Satan as a preliminary condition to Christian service; *sacramenti testatio* is the oath of fidelity to Christ; anointing is priestly consecration; milk and honey signify fruition of the new land of promise. In these examples one notices the natural pliability of borrowed elements. They easily lend themselves to Christian interpretation. In other words, they possess a certain "connaturality" to express the Christian mystery. Obviously their introduction into the Christian liturgy could lead neophytes to misinterpretation or bad theology. To avoid confusion the Fathers always insisted on the need for catechesis. Sometimes they went so far as to ignore the cultural dimensions of these rituals. This has left us groping in the forgotten past for their historical origin. But the attempt at adaptation during this period was so successful that the Church kept many of its re-

sults. Canonization has been her way of showing approval.
Thus Christian liturgy, which is rooted in the Jewish cult, is at
the same time profoundly influenced by Greco-Roman culture
which was already at work in this early stage of ritual forma-
tion. Many local churches without any Greco-Roman background ignore this and start, as it were, from the original
apostolic tradition. The question is not simply a matter of
method but of attitude to history and tradition.

One cannot dwell on this period without mentioning its
features of improvisation and spontaneity. The missal and sacramentaries as we know them today did not exist, and there
was no way except to improvise the prayers. This does not
mean that there was no definite outline of the eucharistic
prayer, for instance. It means that the actual formulation and
length of the prayer were left to the discretion of the leader.
The *Didaché*, which offers prayer formulas for the *agape* or
perhaps the eucharistic celebration, adds afterward that the
prophets should be allowed to give thanks as much as they
willed. Justin Martyr relates that the president of the eucharistic assembly recited a long prayer of thanksgiving to the
best of his ability.[62] Hippolytus of Rome, who composed a eucharistic prayer and other liturgical formulas, reminds the
bishop that it is not necessary to pray in those words or to repeat them from memory. Each one may pray according to his
gifts and talents, in an elaborate and solemn manner or simply and briefly. His compositions were not meant to be fixed
formulas but models. That is why he does not oblige the bishop
to recite the same words, although he insists that the sense of
the prayer be kept. But the ultimate norm, according to him,
is the rule of faith. The bishop may improvise and pray extem-
poraneously, but his prayer must conform to orthodox doctrine.[63]

Adaptation from the Edict of Milan
to the Seventh Century

The advent of the Constantinian era has had a profound
and lasting effect on Christianity. Free at last, and now a state

religion, Christianity let loose its pent-up vigor and advanced with giant strides into every home, institution, village and city of the Greco-Roman world. This period saw the flowering of patristic theology and the insertion of the Church into the cultural and socio-political streams of ancient civilization. All this had a profound influence on the development and future shape of the liturgy. From an intimate household celebration the liturgy evolved into something both solemn and regal in the splendor of Constantinian basilicas.[64] Not only the Roman rite but also the different Oriental rites began to flourish and attain their specific forms toward the seventh century.[65] In the case of Christian initiation we witness the development of a magnificent ritual which was a far cry from the simplicity Tertullian was boasting about between the years 200 and 206.[66] One who reads the mystagogical catechesis of Cyril of Jerusalem or of Ambrose of Milan is impressed by the solemnity and grandeur of initiation rite held during the Easter vigil.[67]

Creativity and adaptation characterize this period. Needless to say, Scripture remains as the principal source of inspiration for the composition of liturgical texts. The mystagogical catecheses of Cyril of Jerusalem and the homilies of Ambrose of Milan to neophytes are some of the finest examples of how Scripture thoroughly permeates the liturgy.[68] Biblical themes centering on the history of salvation are the veins of the eucharistic prayers composed during this period. These are prayers of praise and thanksgiving to God for the work of creation and for the promise of salvation and its realization in Christ.[69]

Attachment to traditional forms is easily discernible, notwithstanding the frenzy of creation and adaptation. Thus the model in the construction of Constantinian basilicas is no other than the *domus ecclesiae:* not a temple where God dwells, but a royal and festive hall where the Christian community gathers to listen to the Word of God and celebrate the Eucharist.[70] At the apse of the basilica is the seat of the president of the assembly (the bishop), surrounded by a semi-circle of benches for the presbyters.[71] In the sanctuary are the lectern for the Word of God and a portable (?) table for the Eucharist.[72] The nave is ample space for the faithful and catechumens.[73] In short, the Constantinian basilica is an enlarged and highly stylized *domus ecclesiae.*

But this period also shows two striking features. The antagonism to pagan cult gradually softened and finally turned to open acceptance.[74] On the other hand, the Church became less and less interested in assimilating cultural elements with no strictly cultic significance. The rite of initiation in the fourth and fifth centuries does not show any new acquisition. Rites like renunciation, profession of faith, anointing and the kiss of peace (milk and honey disappeared) were retained and became traditional elements of initiation. But their cultural provenance seems to have been erased from the Church's memory. In explaining the pre-baptismal anointing, Ambrose had to allude to the athlete and his hardships in the arena to win the crown.[75] John Chrysostom had to refer to the oath that slaves swore to their new masters in order to explain the meaning of baptismal profession.[76] This seems to imply that the secular origin of these rites was no longer obvious.

In the baptismal rite of Ambrose there is a detail which may give a clue to the changed attitude of the Church toward social rituals. The practice of washing the feet of neophytes was common among Gallican liturgies until the fourth century.[77] It must have been incorporated in the rite of initiation in earlier centuries as a sign of welcome to neophytes.[78] The liturgy, of course, interpreted it in the context of the Last Supper of Jesus, although such an interpretation is little warranted. The rite continued to be observed in Milan in the time of Ambrose, but Rome had not known the practice and did not approve of it. However, Ambrose would not be encroached upon. In a lapidary statement he outlined the principle of pluralism within ecclesial communion: "I desire to follow the Roman Church in everything, but we also possess our own feeling. Therefore, what others rightly observe elsewhere we also rightly observe here."[79]

What was the objection of Rome against washing the feet of neophytes? Ambrose surmised that the practice declined in other churches because of the large number of candidates. But there was another reason which reveals an attitude of suspicion toward social rituals. "There are some who do not want it," explains Ambrose, "declaring that while it is fitting to wash the feet of guests, it is not fitting to do it in the course of the mystery, of baptism, of regeneration."[80] The washing of feet was too secular a custom to be incorporated into so sacred and holy a mystery. It was not fear of pagan cult that held the Church, but fear of mundane contamination. At this time the Church seems to have begun "sacralizing" her liturgy, the liturgy that she formerly guarded so zealously from altars and temples, from anything that smelled of incense and burning candles.

This does not mean, however, that from the fourth century on the Church abandoned the practice of assimilating purely cultural or socio-political elements into the liturgy. While the rite of Christian initiation exhibits no new "secular" acquisition, other areas of the liturgy continued to acquire them. It is well known that pontifical ceremonials of this period were adapted from those of the imperial court.[81] Liturgical vestments, which have undergone numerous changes, elaborations and stylizations down the Christian centuries, were originally the Roman *tunica, paenula,* or *toga* and *mappula.*[82] Christianity's attitude toward culture was one of respect for what it found noble and wholesome in human society. In this period we witness the Church's incarnation in the non-Jewish world. It was at this time that the Church in the land of the Romans began to be a Roman Church.

A most interesting example of contact between Christian liturgy and the socio-political structure of the period is the Sacramentary of Verona's prayers of ordination of bishops, presbyters and deacons.[83] In these prayers one constantly meets terms like *honor, dignitas,* and *gradus.* In the Roman socio-political milieu *honor* was the respect and esteem given by the people to a public officer; it is the consequence of installation or promotion to an office.[84] The office itself with its various ranks was considered a dignitas, as in *dignitas senatoria.*[85] Dignity in this sense indicated the worth or value of both the office and its holder. In the age of Constantine clerics acquired

civil dignity, so that bishops and presbyters were ranked as
civil dignitaries with all the honors accorded to state dignitaries.[86] The Sacramentary takes this situation into account
and incorporates it in its texts, although under a new perspective. Sacerdotal dignity, rank and honor originate from God
himself who is their *distributor*. The person on whom they are
conferred must consequently use them for the greater glory
and service of their giver. On the other hand, *gradus* in the Roman socio-political system were the various stages one had to
ascend in the course of a public career. *Sacerdotalis gradus,*
applied to presbyters, indicates that the presbyterate is the
first step of ascent to priestly hierarchy which culminates in
the episcopate. However, unlike the Sacramentary's concep-
tion of diaconate, the presbyterate does not automatically rise
up to the episcopate. Presbyteral rank simply implies the superiority of the *gradus episcoporum*. It is in the case of deacons
that the idea of promotion in the ecclesiastical rank becomes
very pronounced. Diaconate is a transitional stage in a cleric's
gradual ascent *ad potiora*. Here the Sacramentary stresses its
version of ecclesiastical hierarchy with its various degrees or
ranks after the pattern of the Constantinian socio-political
system. Unlike Hippolytus' concept of diaconate as *gradus
magnus et excelsus,*[87] the diaconate of this Sacramentary is an
inferior gradus which finds its fulfillment in the *potior gradus*
of the presbyterate.[88]

But very much in the tradition of the Fathers, the Sacramentary of Verona does not borrow from Constantinianism
without the process of purification through biblical typology.
It justifies its cultural acquisitions by searching for anti-types
in the *enigmata figurarum* and the *velamina* of the Old Testament. The *habitus* of the Old Testament priest is interpreted
as the spiritual adornment of the bishop, and the *honor ves-
tium* that once extolled the Jewish high priest is now the
splendor animorum which commends and manifests the *ponti-
ficalis gloria* of the bishop. The ecclesiastical ranking itself is
seen by the Sacramentary as divinely instituted *per ordinem
congrua ratione dispositum* in view of man's spiritual growth.
Indeed the various gradus in the Church are *varietas caeles-*

tium gratiarum. It is difficult to dismiss the influence of the Constantinian socio-political system in these prayers, even if these interpret dignity, honor and rank in a spiritual and liturgical manner.[89]

The other striking feature of this period is the striking behavior of the Church toward pagan cults. In contrast to the preceding centuries she regarded them now as possible storehouses of her liturgical rites. This change of attitude should be seen within the historical framework of the period. By the time of Nicea, the Church began to learn the delicate art of compromise with pagan cults, a compromise dictated by the new situation. Her new members were no longer merely pagan Jewish sympathizers or synagogue frequenters; they were pagans with a thoroughly pagan background. These were Gentiles who were raised in the milieu of temples, idols, mystery rites, sacrifices and pagan religious festivities. Although pagan worship was officially interdicted by Emperor Theodosius in 378, it would be naive to imagine that popular attachment to it disappeared overnight. For a long time the *pagani,* villagers who lived far away from the control of authority, continued to hold idol worship quite undisturbed. But the threat of paganism had been overcome and there was no longer any proximate danger of relapsing into idolatry. This explains the Church's policy in the fourth century. It also explains her policy in similar circumstances. As long as there is danger of idolatry, she shies away from any contact with paganism. But as soon as the danger is removed, she withdraws her declaration of war and lifts the danger sign.

A few random examples can show the extent of pagan religious influence on the liturgy.[90] For a time Christians indulged in the practice of *refrigerium* or meal held by the grave at which a portion of food and drink was set aside for the dead person.[91] The practice degenerated into excessive drinking, and so Ambrose of Milan forbade it, while Augustine of Hippo, who was more tolerant on the matter, turned it to a celebration for charitable purposes.[92] Another example of pagan influence is seen in the Christian prayers of Hellenistic provenance, like the Euchologion of Serapion of Thmuis, which betray linguistic peculiarities proper to pre-Christian Hellenistic prayers of the period.[93] Solemn addresses, numerous divine attributes, especially the negative-positive ones (infinite, ineffable, incomprehensible) and the rhetorical style borrowed from Hellenistic culture abound in these liturgical formulas.[94] Paganism can also be detected in such litanic responses as *Libera nos, Domine* and *Te, rogamus, audi nos,* which are derived from the Roman practice of invoking the divinities with a series of petitionary acclamations. Likewise, kissing the altar and sacred images originated from pagan gestures of reverence.[95] Christian initiation also began to accumulate pagan usages. It becomes fashionable among the Fathers to use terms directly borrowed from mystery rites, such as *memneménoi* (persons initiated into Christian mystery), *mystagogós* (the teacher) and *mystagogía* (his doctrine). Illustrative elements from pagan cults were also incorporated into the Christian rite. The white garment given to neophytes of mystery religions became a distinguishing mark of the Christian initiate.[96] Baptismal candles, alluded to by Gregory of Nazianzus and Gregory of Nyssa in their Easter homilies, further enhanced the solemnity of the celebration.[97] And the practice of turning to the East after the rite of renunciation became a graphic gesture of the catechumen's conversion to Christ.[98] This last element was influenced by the Mediterranean solar religions.[99]

In these examples one can detect two methods of adaptation. One was substitution, the other assimilation. The former was carried out by replacing pagan cultic elements with Christian ones, in such a way that these practically abolished them. In the case of pagan feasts, the Church instituted new feasts celebrating events of salvation history in place of and in opposition to the pagan festivals. The process of substitution had its rationale, for there was a similarity of themes or analogy between the one and the other. One cannot speak here of Christianizing or "baptizing" pagan feasts, but of abolishing them and filling the empty space with Christian celebrations. A well-known case is Christmas, the birth of the true Sun of Justice, replacing the feast of the birth of the sun-god in Mithraic religion. The feast of the Chair of Saint Peter (and of Saint Paul?) on February 22 took the place of the Roman *caristia* or *cara cognatio,* which was a commemoration of the dead ancestors whose authority was represented by their chairs.[100]

By the method of assimilation the Church adopted pagan rituals and gestures into which she could infuse a Christian meaning. Besides the many examples cited above, another interesting example can be mentioned here, that of facing the East during prayer, which was a Mediterranean custom inspired by solar cults.[101] The Arabic and Ethiopian versions of the *Apostolic Tradition* of Hippolytus instruct the baptizand to face the East as he professes faith in the Holy Trinity.[102] The Christian tradition of praying toward the East and of orienting churches toward it is a vestige of a similar custom in solar religions.[103] It should be noted that when such elements were incorporated in the liturgy, they were meant to illustrate the central mystery of the celebration. They correspond to the explanatory rites of today's sacramental celebrations. The post-baptismal anointing,[104] the wearing of white garments,[105] and the giving of lighted candles are explanatory rites which illustrate what has happened during the essential rite of washing with water in the word. These elements are not meant to substitute the apostolic or biblical traditions or dwarf them into insignificance. Being cultural elements, and in the past part and parcel of contemporary culture, they bridge the gap between Scripture and people.

By the seventh century the contact between the liturgy of Rome and the Greco-Roman culture was a *fait accompli.* The socio-political standing of the Bishop of Rome finds resonance in papal liturgy,[106] as pictured for example by the Ordo Romanus I,[107] which minutely describes the solemn stational Mass: the Pope comes from the Lateran on horseback, accompanied by ministers and city officials, enters the basilica with seven acolytes, seven deacons, seven subdeacons, while the choir sings the Introit and so on. It was a liturgy whose expression was solemn, grand and regal. However, after the collection of the gifts of the assembly, the Roman Mass continued in its original simplicity, brevity and sobriety, with few ceremo-

nies and only those which were necessary, like the elevation at
the eucharistic doxology, kiss of peace, breaking of bread and
procession at Communion. Here we find a quality of the Roman rite, which is able to conserve its essential features de-
spite the accumulation of new elements. Because of its
simplicity, brevity and sobriety it was and still is extremely
vulnerable to endless modifications and adaptations.[108] But
subsequent reforms of the Roman liturgy would always center
on a return to the original Roman genius: the Gregorian reform of the eleventh century which demanded a return to the
"pure" Roman form,[109] the Roman Pontificals of the twelfth
century which abbreviated the Franco-Germanic rituals and
made them more practical,[110] the Tridentine attempt (although minimal) to purify the medieval liturgy,[111] the contro-
versial Synod of Pistoia in 1786 which forced the issue in favor
of the original and pure Roman form,[112] and the classical Liturgical Movement and Vatican II which revived quite effectively the Roman liturgy of the classical period.[113] These
examples manifest the inner dynamism of the Roman liturgy,
which is able to recover its proper features from the accumula-
tions and encumbrances of centuries. At the same time, they
are significant for adaptation, for they show that there is a
certain limit to the assimilation of cultural elements in the liturgy. This limit is imposed by the nature of the liturgy in general and by the features proper to the genius of the Roman
rite in particular.

Another important feature of this period is its tendency to
bring about a relative homogeneity among different liturgical
rites. One may have suspected that the movement would have
been from unity to diversity. But history moved from diversity
to relative uniformity.[114] The improvisation and spontaneity
of the earlier centuries which fostered liturgical pluralism
was gradually being abandoned in favor of fixed formularies.[115] Liturgical texts began to be put into writing and collect-
ed into what we know today as the Sacramentary,[116]
Lectionary,[117] Antiphonary[118] and *Ordines Romani,*[119] the
last one being a description of liturgical rites. Nor was the cre-
ative activity of this period exactly what one may term *creatio*

ex nihilo.[120] The flow of communication among churches promoted closer ties not only in doctrinal formulation but also in liturgical forms.[121] Alexandria borrowed several liturgical elements from Antioch,[122] while Ethiopia translated Greek texts.[123] In the fourth century Rome adopted the Oriental feast of the Epiphany.[124] It incorporated the Kyrie (with invocations) in the Mass after the fifth century,[125] and the *Gloria* before the sixth century.[126] The letter of Pope Gregory the Great to Augustine of Canterbury probably typifies the attitude of the Roman Church at this time.[127] Augustine, who was quite resentful of the independence of the bishops of Gaul, complained to Gregory about the lack of uniformity among different Churches in the celebration of the Mass.[128] Quite unexpectedly the Pope manifested no apprehension at Gaul's non-conformity with the liturgy of the Roman Church, but instead directed the apostle of England to adapt from any Church, whether of Rome, Gaul or any other, those usages which could be beneficial to the young Church:

Novit fraternitas tua Romanae ecclesiae consuetudinem in qua se meminit nutritam: valde amabilem (eam) habeat. Sed mihi placet ut sive Romana, sive in Galliarum sive in qualibet ecclesia aliquid invenisti quod plus omnipotenti Deo possit placere sollicite eligat et in Anglorum ecclesia, quae adhuc ad fidem nova est, institutionem praecipuam quam de multis ecclesiis colligare potuit, infundat. Non enim pro locis res sed pro bonis rebus loca amanda sunt. Ex singulis ergo quibusque ecclesiis quae pia, quae recta sunt eligat et haec quasi in vasculo collecta apud Anglorum mensa in consuetudinem depone.

You, brother, know the usage of the Roman Church in which you were brought up: hold it very much in affection. But as far as I am concerned, if you have found something more pleasing to Almighty God, either in the Roman or in the Frankish or in any other Church, make a careful choice and institute in the Church of the English—which as yet is new to the faith—the best usages which you have gathered together from many Churches. For we should love things not because of the places where they are found, but places because of the good things they contain. Therefore choose from each particular Church what is godly, religious and sound, and gathering all together as it were into a dish, place it on the table of the English for their customary diet.[129]

Gregory was advocating a free exchange of liturgical customs and traditions among churches. Fidelity to liturgical tradition was not synonymous with fidelity to the Roman rite. Gregory was aware that the pure Roman liturgy did not necessarily suit the cultural taste and needs of the peoples of Gaul and England. Young churches did not have to take exclusively from a single liturgical form, for no one possessed all the qualities which would satisfy the particular demands of every nation. Thus, the Gallican rite, whose remote origins seem to have been Rome itself,[130] was already richly embellished with Byzantine elements (*trisagion,* litanies, offertory entrance)[131] before its suppression by Pepin, the father of Charlemagne.[132] From these examples one can see that the Church during this period not only adapted cultural elements into the liturgy, but also borrowed existing liturgical practices from other rites. Creativity must be tempered by tradition, and pluralism must be guided by unity. Vatican II's Constitution on the Sacred Liturgy, article 23, reflects this principle, when it states that "care must be taken that any new forms adopted should in some way grow organically from forms already existing."

Adaptation from the Eighth Century to the Age of the Baroque

By the seventh century the different liturgical rites in both East and West had acquired their basic shape and characteristics. Of special interest for the history of adaptation is the fate of the Roman rite when it "migrated" to the land of the Franco-Germanic people in the eighth century. It did not take long before it yielded to the pressures of the new cultural world it entered. Rituals once austere were adorned by drama and elaborate ceremonials.[133] Prayer texts once direct and simple were adorned with a flourish and approached verbosity. The *praefacio* of the *Missa in vigilia Paschae* of the *Missale Gallicanum Vetus* (ninth century) is a notable example of

Franco-Germanic elaboration of a simple, brief and sober Roman prayer:

Sacr. Greg.-Had	*Missale Gallicanum Vetus*
Deus	Omnipotens sempiterne Deus,
qui hanc sacratissimam noctem	qui hanc sacratissimam noctem
	per universa mundi spacia
gloria dominicae resur-	gloria dominicae resur-
rectionis inlustras	rectionis inlustras,
conserva in novam familiae	conserva in novam familiae
tuae progeniem	tuae progeniem
adoptionis spiritum	sanctificationis spiritum
quem dedisti,	quem dedisti,
ut corpore et mente renovati	ut corpore et mente renovati
puram tibi exhibeant	puram tibi animam et purum
servitutem.[134]	pectus semper exhibeant.[135]

We have a typical example of Gallican flourish here. The direct invocation *Deus* is elaborated to *Omnipotens sempiterne Deus*. The anamnestic prodosis acquires an expansive mood with the addition of *per universa mundi spacia*. And in line with the Franco-Germanic moralizing tendency, *adoptionis spiritum* is changed to *sanctificationis spiritum*, while the phrase *puram servitutem* becomes *puram animam et purum pectus*. Thus the concise and theological Roman formula is transformed into the elaborate and moralistic Franco-Germanic prayer. Adaptation in this case should probably not be considered as theological impoverishment of the Roman original,[136] but rather as an attempt to translate it to the religious culture of the northerners.

Around the year 783 Charlemagne requested Pope Hadrian I to send him a copy of a pure Roman Sacramentary for the uniform use of his empire, which was beset by liturgical "anarchy."[137] The Sacramentary arrived two years later and was exhibited at the library of Aachen as the *liber authenticus*. It proved, however, to be defective. Mass formularies after Epiphany, during the Octaves of Easter and Pentecost, funeral rite, rite of reconciliation, votive Masses and blessings were missing altogether. To remedy the situation, which must have been quite embarrassing for the emperor, Alcuin (or Benedict of Aniane?) had to add supplementary texts taken from Gallican usages, such as blessing of the Easter candle, ordinations, blessings, dedication of churches and exorcisms.[138] These additions were at first a distinct supplement to the Roman Sacramentary, but were later incorporated in the Sacramentary itself, resulting in a Roman-Franco-Germanic hybrid.[139] Thus, not only did they supply what was lacking in the Roman Sacramentary, but they also effectively adapted it to a people who had special preference for the dramatic, the verbose and the moralizing. In Mainz toward the year 950 the Ordines Romani were elaborated with elements borrowed from the sacramentaries to form the *Pontificale Romano-Germanicum* of the tenth century.[140] The sermons, expositions, blessings, exorcisms and ordeals (!) which were incorporated in this liturgical book adapted it to the taste of the northerners of this period.[141] This particular period shows that, because of its simplicity, brevity, sobriety and practicality, the classical form of the Roman liturgy can be easily adapted to practically any culture and tradition, including those which have little in common with the Roman genius. The program of adaptation outlined by SC 37–40 can look back to this period for its model. By bringing back the Roman rite to its classical form, the Council facilitated the task of adaptation. It offered to various cultures and traditions a liturgical form which can be further elaborated according to their proper expressions. What the Franco-Germanic people did to the Roman liturgy after it "migrated" to the north can similarly be done today by others.

But it was also a period of great literary and poetic compositions (*Veni Creator, Victimae paschali laudes, Ut queant laxis*)[142] as well as of magnificent Romanesque churches in Germany, France and Spain.[143] Other features of this period, such as the decline of active participation, private Masses,[144] devotions to saints, private prayers during Mass and the obsession to repeatedly confess one's sins during Mass *(apologiae)* are well known.[145] During its sojourn in the north the Roman rite easily adapted itself to the genius and sensitivity of the people, sometimes at the cost of sacrificing its own genius and tradition. Decadent features, however, need not be imputed to the Franco-Germanic people, but should be blamed on the general religious culture of the period.[146] At any rate, the contact of the Roman rite with the northern people did not cause irreparable damages. Indeed the new culture endowed it with a freshness and vitality which Rome did not hesitate to appropriate in the tenth century, when it returned to Rome in its hybrid form as Roman Franco-Germanic liturgy.

The medieval period between the tenth and the thirteenth century can be rightly regarded as one of the more outstanding epochs in the history of the Church.[147] It was the age of powerful emperors and conquerors, like the Ottonian emperors who brought the Roman Franco-Germanic liturgy back to Rome, Stephen of Hungary, El Cid and Frederick Barbarosa. It was the age of Crusades and crusaders, and of monastic reforms such as Cluny, Chartreuse and Citeaux. Of interest to the history of adaptation was the attempt of Pope Gregory VII to return to the *ordinem romanum et antiquum morem.*[148] It was the first attempt to restore the classical form of the Roman liturgy. While Gregory VII succeeded in imposing discipline on the Roman clergy, he failed in his intention of "purifying" the Roman liturgy of its northern elements. The *apologiae,* private prayers of the priest during Mass and new signs of eucharistic reverence remained. More successful was the work of the Roman liturgists of the twelfth century, who shortened and simplified the *Pontificale Romano-Germanicum* of the tenth century by eliminating didactic explanations and such rituals as ordeals and exorcisms of persons possessed by evil spirits. These things did not appeal to the Roman sense of sobriety.[149] However, the twelfth century emphasis on eucharistic theology brought about new practices revolving around the moment of consecration: multiple gestures of reverence,[150] and the use of bells and candles.[151] The next century saw the flowering of Christian spirituality, monumental Scholastic writings and the rise of the great cathedrals of Europe (Rheims, La Sainte Chappelle, Burgos, Wells and Assisi).[152] A significant liturgical reform of the period was the one initiated by Pope Innocent III (1198–1216) who codified the common usages of the Roman Church for the use of his curia. Although the result tended toward the Roman classical form, it was tinged with legalism, allegorism and pietism.[153] It was this thirteenth century liturgy which the Friar Minors propagated throughout the world through their missionary activity.[154]

The Liturgical Movement's and Vatican II's insistence to return to the classical form of the Roman liturgy is thus not a novelty in liturgical history. The Roman Church has always had a great respect for its classical tradition. The difference between the reform from the eleventh to the thirteenth century and the reform of Vatican II lies in the intention of the Council to make the liturgy more available and accessible to various cultures and traditions. Adaptations must be based on the authentic Roman form rather than on local modifications of the Roman liturgy.

The fourteenth, fifteenth and part of the sixteenth centuries mark the autumn of the Middle Ages and the decline of liturgical life.[155] But it is not a period that can be easily disregarded, for it possessed a feature which touched on liturgical adaptation. It was at this time that the dramatization of the liturgy flourished in many European countries and continued to flourish until the Baroque period.[156] Not that the earlier centuries did nothing of the sort. Some of these liturgical plays existed already in the twelfth century, but drama had not been as important an element of public worship as it was during this period.[157] The plays re-enacted the events commemorated by liturgical feasts, sometimes incorporating apocryphal stories[158] with a view to adding more savor to the drama. They were performed in church at the beginning of or even during the Mass itself.[159] The texts were basically those of the Mass and the Divine Office. It was only after indecorous and comic skits crept in that many such plays were evicted from the church to the marketplaces where they were decidedly transformed into buffoonery. The original liturgical plays revolved around the Christmas story, Holy Week, Corpus Christi and the Blessed Virgin. Through the Spanish missionaries some of them[160] reached Latin America and the Philippines where they still survive in a modified state. Examples of these are the Christmas star that moves through the nave of the church to the crib at the sanctuary during the Gloria of Midnight Mass, passion plays and the meeting of Christ and his Mother at Easter dawn[161] before Mass.

Liturgical plays flourished during the decadent period, but the official liturgy provided the inspiration. The procession with palms, the dramatic chanting of the passion narrative, the washing of feet, the "entombment" or reposition of the sacred host on Holy Thursday, the veneration of the cross and the reproaches: these are dramatic elements, borrowed by Rome mostly from the north, which paved the way for the growth of liturgical plays. And at a time when the liturgy no longer spoke the language of the people, it was to be expected that pastors, Pope Gregory XI at Avignon included, would welcome liturgical plays as a form of catechetical instruction.[162] But one cannot totally ignore their negative impact on liturgical life. For while they instructed the people on the events commemorated by the liturgy, they did not deepen their understanding of the liturgy itself, but rather stole their attention away from it.

The question of drama in the liturgy is not a thing of the past. While it should not be reintroduced in the liturgy as a substitute to the understanding of liturgical texts and rituals, especially now that the liturgy is in the vernacular, certain cultural exigencies may nevertheless necessitate the revival of drama or at least of dramatic elements in the liturgy.[163] For the Roman simplicity, brevity and sobriety are not always and everywhere admired as human qualities. The motivation, therefore, for introducing drama or dramatic elements in the liturgy is to allow culture to participate in it. Drama should never substitute for proper liturgical catechesis and mystagogy. Nor should catechesis be an excuse for ignoring drama, where culture requires it as part of liturgical celebration and experience.[164]

At the eve of the Protestant Reformation one could observe what J. Jungmann so aptly calls "the flowering of autumn."[165] Religious and liturgical life seemed to flourish: chapels and oratories were built by guilds and rich families, but they were intended for their own worship; there was strong popular piety, but it was subjective and individualistic and with little reference to ecclesial community; the liturgical year received great attention, but the mystery it celebrated (with emphasis on Christmas and the passion) was more of a past event to be contemplated than a present mystery to be participated in. With such state of affairs there was hardly any possibility to celebrate the liturgy, for there was no longer any sense of the worshiping community nor of the presence of the liturgical mystery. As J. Jungmann so pointedly remarked, "There was a mighty façade, and behind it—a great emptiness."[166] Autumn, however, did not come unannounced. The preceding centuries, especially from the tenth to the thirteenth, carried the germ of this unhappy situation: a clerical liturgy, ignorance of the nature of liturgical act, allegorical theology or its opposite (an exaggeratedly realistic theology of "transubstantiation," for example),[167] and the lack of harmony between liturgical language and the popular linguaggio, and between liturgical rites and contemporary culture. History teaches us that when the liturgy is not adapted to the times, does not respond to its demands and lacks solid theological basis, autumn is just around the corner.

The Council of Trent (1545–1563) plays an important role in the history of the Roman liturgy in general, but not of adaptation in particular. Since its principal aim was to curb abuses and institute reforms, it could not be expected to further muddle up the situation by introducing new adaptations in the liturgy.[168] Although liturgy was much discussed, the Council did not come up with any concrete reform of liturgical books. Instead, in the last session (December 3-4, 1563) the Council entrusted to the Pope the revision and promulgation of the Missal and the breviary, *ut eius iudicio atque auctoritate terminetur et evulgetur.*[169] With the establishment of the Sacred Congregation of Rites by Sixtus V in 1588 the centralizing effort of Trent was realized, free development of the liturgy in local churches was ended, and the liturgy came to a stand-still.[170] Centuries rolled on, cultures evolved, and new mission-ary situations arose, but the liturgy of the Roman Church remained inflexible and oblivious of all these factors. Canon Law and moral theology further fortified the wall that protect-ed the liturgy from any new development.[171] Trent's achieve-ments in liturgical reform became a disadvantage in later centuries, because the reform intended for a particular mo-ment in the life of the Church was canonized for the succeed-ing generations. Trent was the best answer to the problems of the time, but it could not be expected to be the best answer to the problems of all times. Indeed, the Tridentine reform was very much in the context of the period. While it codified exist-ing liturgical usages and avoided novelty and archeologism, it purified the Roman rite of its medieval abuses. But codifica-tion eventually alienated it from the people who were forced to take to popular forms of piety and devotion, thus ironically giving birth to the religious culture of the Baroque.

The age of the Baroque reflects the festive mood of a Church celebrating her victory over the chaos of the Middle Ages and the crisis of the Reformation. The liturgy, now re-formed and uniformly observed, was unable, however, to resist the pressures coming from the religious culture of the period: a flair for festivity, external manifestations of grandeur and triumphalism, especially through pilgrimages and processions with banners, and sensuousness in artistic expression and pi-ous devotions. Thus it is perfectly understandable that the feast *par excellence* of the Baroque period should be Corpus Christi with its solemn procession complete with banners, cos-tumes and guards of honor. The church building itself was transformed into the festive hall of the Eucharistic King, into an elaborately decorated salon with an imposing tabernacle, like a throne, resting on the altar.[172] The Mass was conse-quently a celebration whose festivity was heightened by or-chestra and polyphonic music, while the consecration was hailed by band music, jubilant ringing of bells and, in the Phil-ippines, also firecrackers! J. Jungmann remarked, "Because aesthetic consideration began to hold sway, the liturgy was not only submerged under this ever-growing art but actually suppressed, so that even at this time there were festive occasions which might best be described as 'church concerts with liturgical accompaniment.' "[173] The Roman liturgy, although in Latin and according to strict rubrical laws, was celebrated with abandon, merriment and theatrical display. However, active participation in the liturgy was almost nil; the external elements were excessively magnified and the essential dwarfed and relegated to the periphery of the celebration. For many the Mass was an excellent occasion to recite the rosary and perform devotions to patron saints. But notwithstanding these setbacks which need not be considered hopelessly irremediable, it must be admitted that the Baroque way of celebrating the liturgy, at least in its historical situation, corresponded closely to the temperament of the people.[174]

But the externalism of the Baroque form of liturgy should not be blamed entirely on the Baroque culture. The intransigence of Tridentine liturgical reform which excluded practically every possibility of adapting the liturgy to the culture of the period had much to do with the situation. If Vatican II's liturgy should become as inflexible as that of Trent, there would be a real danger of repeating the Baroque experience. Indeed many cultures possess Baroque traits, and it may be advisable to study the possibility of incorporating them in the liturgy in order to modify its classical brevity, simplicity and sobriety in favor of a more exuberant expression.

Adaptation During the Periods of Illuminism, Restoration and Liturgical Movement

The spirit of Illuminism in the eighteenth century found its way into the area of liturgy as a protest against Tridentine centralization and the Baroque externalism. From 1680 until a century later there were attempts to revive the Gallican liturgies through the publication of the Breviary of Paris in 1680, the Breviary of Cluny in 1686, the Breviary and Missal of Paris in 1736 and the Breviary of the Benedictines of St. Maur in 1787.[175] Abstracting from whatever political overtone it possessed, the movement represented a valid desire to return to the original status of liturgical pluralism in the Western Church. Two centuries later Vatican II would recognize the validity and need of such a pluralism on the basis of cultural diversity among local churches. However, the principle of Vatican II was not the revival of ancient liturgies, but the adaptation of the reformed Roman rite to the cultures of today, as SC 37–40 points out. Liturgical pluralism is thus to be understood in the context of the Roman liturgical tradition.

But the more dramatic liturgical reforms were those instituted by the Synod of Pistoia in Tuscany in 1786 and by the Congress of Ems in Germany in the same year. Inspired by patristic tradition, these synods attempted to return to the authentic spirit and form of the Roman liturgy, thus heralding the advent of the Classical Liturgical Movement which began in 1909 and culminated in Vatican II. Contesting the exuberance of the Baroque, the Synod of Pistoia, presided by Bishop Scipione Ricci, decreed, among other things, a return to one altar in church, Communion from species consecrated during the same Mass, active participation, use of the vernacular, reading of the entire Sacred Scripture within the cycle of a year, reform of the breviary, parish celebrations, primacy of Sunday and reform of popular devotions. But because the Synod was tinged with Josephinism and Jansenism, it was condemned by Pius VI in his Apostolic Constitution *Auctorem Fidei*.[176] Because its reform, valid in itself, was practically imposed on clergy and people who were not prepared for it, the Synod was a total failure. History teaches us that adaptation and liturgical renewal can succeed only if ecclesial unity is preserved and the people are formed in the authentic spirit of the liturgy. If Vatican II's liturgical reform, on the other hand, did receive a better response, it was because of the role played by the Classical Liturgical Movement. The similarity between Pistoia and Vatican II is not due to any borrowing on the part of Vatican II, but to the historical and traditional sources which were common to both.

The age of Restoration which A. Meyer severely criticizes as *gnadenloses Jahrhundert* was a reaction to the excess of Illuminism with the sad consequence of a return to the *Ancien régime,* to romanticism, to the Baroque and medieval forms.[177] It was indeed the movement of the pendulum to the extreme right. It is in this context that the work of Abbot P. Guéranger of Solesmes should be evaluated.[178] Successfully averting the revival of Gallican liturgies, he advocated fidelity to the authority of Rome and the preservation of the Tridentine Roman rite together with its sacred and "mysterious" language.[179] However, a more balanced judgment on the activity of Abbot Guéranger in this period of religious indifferentism, anticlericalism, liberalism, atheism, materialism and communism has still to be written.[180] He was a man who was able to stand up against the tempest of his time. But the age of Restoration was not without grace, as far as the history of liturgy and its contribution to liturgical reform are concerned. If adaptation, as SC 37 outlines it, must take into account the authentic spirit of the liturgy, one is compelled to return to the Fathers and to liturgical tradition. And this has been made possible through the monumental works of the period (Migne, Henry Bradshaw Society and Analecta Hymnica) and the scholarship of writers and researchers like F. Probst, A. Ebner, E. Bishop and L. Duchesne. Thus, in its own way the era of Restoration paved the way to a deeper and more solid understanding of the nature and history of the Roman liturgy. Such an understanding is obviously basic to the adaptation envisaged by Vatican II.

The Classical Liturgical Movement has been described by Pius XII as "a sign of the providential dispositions of God in our time, as a movement (*transitus*) of the Holy Spirit in his Church."[181] Initiated by L. Beauduin of Mont-César in Belgium during the Congress of Malines in 1909, the movement espoused a return to the classical form of the Roman liturgy through historical and theological research on liturgical tradition, motivated by pastoral zeal.[182] In the span of fifty years the Church prepared herself for the writing of the Magna Carta of the liturgy, Vatican II's *Sacrosanctum Concilium,* promulgated by Paul VI on December 4, 1963.[183] Thanks to the Liturgical Movement, Vatican II was able to open the door to liturgical adaptation, spell out its principles and, by returning to the original simplicity and clarity of the Roman rite, offer the possibility of adapting it to various cultures and traditions.

The Chinese Rites Controversy

Much has been written on this controversy which raged for over a hundred years and had a traumatic effect on the Roman Church.[184] It began after the death of Matteo Ricci in 1610 and became a closed book only with the publication of the papal bull *Ex quo singulari* in 1742.[185] It involved two great religious orders in the Far East, the Dominicans and the Jesuits, and five Popes: Innocent X, Alexander VII, Clement IX, Clement XI and Benedict XIV. It was a painful experience and a tragedy, for it spelled the loss of China and Indochina to the Church.

The chief aspects of the quarrel were the Jesuit missionaries' use of Chinese words to express the Christian concepts and the permission they granted to their converts to perform, under certain restrictions, the rites in honor of Confucius and their ancestors. Unlike the missionaries in the neighboring Philippines who quite simply foisted Spanish words like *Dios* and *gracia* upon the natives,[186] the Jesuits in China sought terms which approximated Christian concepts and infused them with Christian meaning through catechesis. The question of rites, however, was something that struck at the very heart of the Chinese people.[187] The rite in honor of one's ancestors was the Chinese expression of filial devotion, a virtue which everyone cherished and valued above all else.[188] To wooden tablets bearing the names of the ancestors the Chinese directed ceremonial acts expressing reverence, and offered food, flowers and incense.[189] The Great Teacher, Confucius, was also shown a ritual obeisance. There were two rites in his honor, a simple one which did not differ much from ancestral rite, and a solemn one, reserved to philosophers or scholars, which displayed, according to the judgment of the Dominicans, traits of idolatry and religious sacrifice.[190] The Jesuits forbade this kind of ceremony to their converts, but allowed ancestral worship, provided that no prayers of petitions were directed to the dead, and that the converts rejected the belief that the spirits of ancestors dwelt in the tablets and derived sustenance from food offerings. The Jesuits also made adaptations in the ancestral tablets by inserting the sign of the cross with the instruction: "Worship the true Lord, Creator of heaven, earth and all things, and show filial piety to ancestors and parents."[191] Missionaries from Manila who saw the converts perform the rites denounced the Jesuits for this act of idolatry. What transpired after this is now part of the stormy history of the Church's missionary policy in the Far East. An interesting feature is the instruction penned by Propaganda Fide in 1659 under Alexander VII.[192] It reminded the Vicars Apostolic to China of the absurdity of transplanting Europe to China. The text reads in part: "*Quid enim absurdius quam Galliam, Hispaniam, Italiam aut ullam Europae partem in Synas invehere? Non haec sed fidem importate quae nullius gentis ritus aut consuetudines, quae modo prava non sint, aut respuit aut laedit, immo vero sarta tecta esse vult.*" The Instruction laid down principles of cultural adaptation in the missions. It neatly distinguished between faith and its European cultural expressions, and declared that faith does not repudiate nor destroy the rites and customs of any people, provided they are not perverse. Indeed, says the Instruction, faith wants them to be preserved intact, in order, no doubt, to make use of them as cultural vehicles of the Christian message in these places. Unfortunately the significance of this Instruction was muffled in the height of the controversy and was not resuscitated until 1939 when Pius XII re-echoed it in his encyclical letter *Summi Pontificatus.*[193] It was through this encyclical letter that the Instruction made its way into Vatican II's SC 37.

In 1939 the case was reviewed by Propaganda Fide which published the instruction *Plane compertum,* allowing the Chinese Christians to participate actively in ancestral rites, if these were clearly social affairs devoid of cultic significance, and passively, if they were found superstitious.[194] This change of policy, explains the Congregation, was brought about by the fact that in the course of time the ancestral rites had become merely social with no religious meaning. Or as the *Documentation catholique* commented, "The atmosphere which had been impregnated in the preceding centuries by superstitious beliefs has been cleared and transformed by the secularism and freedom of the religion imported from the West."[195] The permission as such would have been welcome, except that it came too late, for soon China would fall to Communism. But the reasons presented by both Propaganda Fide and the commentary are debatable. Was it a fact that in 1939 the Chinese no longer regarded their ancestral worship as religious cult? Is the distinction between active and passive participation realistic? The underlying motivation for the Church's hesitation regarding the ancestral rites is obviously the Christian traditional attitude of antagonism to pagan rites. History shows that whenever the Church is a minority surrounded by the forces of paganism, as happened during the first four centuries, she would tend to reject any contact with pagan rites. The same phenomenon can be verified in missionary situations, where the converts themselves refuse to adopt pagan rituals and even architecture to Christian cult.[196] Hence, it is understandable that the Church acted the way she did during the Chinese ancestral rite controversy. The problem, however, was the fact that in this case the Chinese converts could not be persuaded to abandon the ancestral rites, for these were part and parcel of their life as a people.

But the Church's antagonism to pagan cult has not been consistently observed in every period of history. According to concrete cultural exigencies the Church modified her stand. One may therefore not take her policy before the fourth century as the only policy. At any rate, it is quite unrealistic to secularize pagan rituals before elevating them to the dignity of Christian worship. The method of secularization in order to sacralize later has no precedent in the history of adaptation. As J. Dourne exclaims, not without mockery, "O blessed secularism that illumines the darkness of paganism."[197]

Ten Years after the Constitution on the Sacred Liturgy

Coinciding with the tenth year of the Constitution on the Sacred Liturgy, the Third Synod of Bishops was held in Rome from September 27 to October 26, 1974. In his report, Cardinal James Knox, Prefect of the Sacred Congregation for the Sacraments and Divine Worship, affirmed that the first phase of Vatican II's liturgical renewal has been realized, since practically all the important liturgical books have been revised.[198] The second phase, however, which is the adaptation of these books to various cultures, will be the concern of the following years henceforth.[199]

Adaptation is an on-going process which cannot be halted, because the life of the Church and the evolution of cultures are in perpetual motion. But this does not mean that changes in the liturgy are to be left to chance or blind fate. The liturgy, like the faith and life it celebrates, is bound to history. It is bound to its Jewish origin, reinterpreted by Jesus Christ and faithfully transmitted by the apostles to the Church. And although bound to Judaism, it did not hesitate to borrow, at an early stage, from the riches of the Greco-Roman world. In every epoch the liturgy incarnated itself for good or ill in the culture of the period, sometimes with great benefit, at other times with consequent loss of authenticity.

History is able to guide the Church by the power of the Holy Spirit toward greater fidelity; history is able to reveal to the Church the models to be imitated and the errors to be avoided. Without profound knowledge of her liturgical history, the Church is condemned to repeat her mistakes. It is not whim that led Vatican II to renew her liturgy with an eye on history and tradition. It is not an exaggeration to affirm that history has offered the Church a fresher appreciation of the theology and pastoral dimension of the mystery she celebrates in her liturgy.

II
The Magna Carta of
Liturgical Adaptation

Vatican II's program of liturgical renewal is outlined in the Constitution on the Liturgy (SC), art. 37–40. The underlying motive of the renewal was to restore the liturgy to its Roman genius of simplicity of structure and clarity of expression in order to promote active and intelligent participation. At the same time the Council wanted to give the Roman liturgy the semblance of universal rite. For indeed most of the churches in the West and in the third world belong to the Roman Rite.[1] It was therefore necessary to offer a liturgy that is truly simple and clear. One can say that the post-conciliar liturgy is one that is flexible enough to admit variations according to different cultures. This is probably the most striking feature of today's Roman rite.

But the question which engages local churches, especially in the third world, is what to do with the new rite. It was not enough to follow simply all its ritual directives. That would be nothing more than a Tridentine mentality wrapped in the new look of Vatican II. Indeed it would be quite contrary to the spirit of the Council. The new rite is a model and is intended for the entire world using the Roman liturgy. This means that it has to be adapted to the particular genius of every local church. Without sacrificing the essential message of the liturgy, the Roman rite has to give way to new cultural expressions, to reinterpretations, modifications and variations. A universal Roman rite means unity in essentials and diversity in cultural forms. The Roman genius marked by simplicity and clarity is not necessarily consistent with the genius of every people. The Roman culture is not a universal culture. However, the essential message of the Roman rite and the program of reform initiated by Vatican II have a universal and lasting value.

SC 21 distinguishes those liturgical elements which are immutable because of divine institution from those which are subject to change. "These latter not only may, but ought to be changed with the passage of time if they have suffered from the intrusion of anything out of harmony with the inner nature of the liturgy or have become unsuited to it." SC 34 further specifies that in the revision of the liturgy the rites should be distinguished by noble simplicity, brevity and clarity. These in fact were some of the characteristics of the Roman liturgy during its classical period from the fifth to the eighth century, before it migrated to the Franco-Germanic regions. The Classical Liturgical Movement which can be said to have culminated in Vatican II urged the return to the classical Roman form, purifying it as much as possible of medieval accretions. Although the revised liturgical books of Vatican II have not always fully succeeded in putting this into effect, they are generally distinguished by simplicity, brevity, sobriety and practicality.

The liturgical adaption foreseen by SC is creativity based on the reformed Roman liturgy. In SC 37–40 are contained the norms for adapting the Roman liturgy to the culture and traditions of peoples.[2] These articles are to be read in the context of other articles of SC, particularly 23 and 24. SC 23 says, "Care must be taken that any new forms adopted should in some way grow organically from forms already existing." The observance of this principle should lead to the ramification of the Roman liturgy into other liturgies which are more suited to other cultures. It should be possible to speak of a Roman liturgical family wherein each new member claims an affinity to both the theological and the formal elements of the Roman liturgy, but is distinguished from it by its cultural expressions.

SC 23 speaks of retention of sound tradition and, at the same time, of openness to legitimate progress. To this effect, it requires, in the spirit of the Classical Liturgical Movement, a theological, historical and pastoral investigation into each part of the liturgy which is to be revised (SC 21). Furthermore, recent liturgical reforms and indults are to be taken into account, and the good of the Church and the process of historical development of liturgical forms should be guaranteed in instituting liturgical changes. SC 34, on the other hand, requires that the rites should be distinguished by the genius of the classical Roman liturgy, namely simplicity, brevity, clarity and practicality.[3] Adaptation therefore presupposes a return to the classical form whence changes and modifications can ensue.[4]

SC 37–40 however made a step farther by allowing the adaptation of the Roman liturgy to the various cultures of peoples. By presenting it in its pure and authentic form, the Council facilitated the work of adaptation. The intention of returning to classical form was thus not for the sake of historical romanticism, but for the sake of providing a liturgical form that could be effectively adapted to the culture of various peoples. What the Franco-Germanic peoples did to the Roman liturgy after the eighth century can similarly be done today by others, especially in the missions.

SC 37: General Principles of Adaptation

This article is based on Pope Pius XII's encyclical letter *Summi Pontificatus*. An analysis of the text reveals that different hands were at work in its final formulation. SC 37 was a delicate issue, as far as the unity of the Roman rite was concerned. Interventions from the floor led to important revisions which made of this article a masterpiece of Vatican II's liturgical policies. Should the Council open the door to pluralism? SC 37 advocates it and invokes no less than the authority of

Pope Pius XII, part of whose encyclical letter *Summi Pontificatus* it reproduces:

Summi Pontificatus

a. Iesu Christi Ecclesia ... ad unitatem contendit ...; non vero ad unam assequendam rerum omnium aequabilitatem, externam tantummodo atque insitas vires debilitantem.

b. Et curas omnes ac normas ... quae quidem ex occultis cuiusque stirpis latebris oriuntur, Ecclesia approbat maternisque votis prosequitur.

c. Quidquid in populorum moribus indissolubili vinculo superstitionibus erroribusque non adstipulatur, benevole non tempore perpenditur ac, si potest sartum tectumque servatur.[5]

SC 37

a. Ecclesia, in iis quae fidem aut bonum totius communitatis non tangunt, rigidam unius tenoris formam ne in liturgia quidem imponere cupit.

b. Quinimmo, variarum gentium populorumque animi ornamenta ac dotes colit et provehit.

c. Quidquid vero in populorum moribus indissolubili vinculo superstitionibus erroribusque non adstipulatur, benevole perpendit ac, si potest, sartum tectumque servat.[6]

The encylical declared that the Church should strive after unity, not mere external uniformity. Inspired by it, the conciliar text states: "Even in the liturgy, the Church has no wish to impose a rigid uniformity in matters which do not involve the faith or the good of the community." The encyclical added that the Church approved of and fostered with maternal concern the gifts which arose from the deepest resources of every race. This the conciliar text paraphrased, declaring that the Church respects the genius and talents of various races and peoples. The affinity of SC 37 to the encyclical letter becomes more pronounced in the following sentence which was lifted from it word for word: "Anything in their way of life that is not indissolubly bound up with superstition and error she studies with sympathy and, if possible, preserves intact."

The phrase "with sympathy" (*benevole* in Latin) was omitted in the proposed text. It could not have been an oversight, since in the climate that obtained in the Conciliar Commission sympathy was not a virtue but an air of superiority. The third world which has been a grateful recipient of Western economic benevolence would have been offended by the Church's demonstration of sympathy for its cultures. Understandably the Commission was apologetic for the reinsertion of the word in the final text: it was to show more clearly that the text had been borrowed from the encyclical letter of Pope Pius XII.[7] For good or ill, the word is there and must be explained, lest this sterling document be marred by the tone of condescension caused by the Council fathers' preoccupation for accurate citation.

Up to this point the proposed text was advocating an attitude of respect and support for traditions and cultures. But as one Council father aptly remarked, it did not give the complete picture of what the Church should propose to herself. It was not enough to proclaim her commitment; it was also necessary to outline her future options and course of action.[8] Thus one of the most revolutionary declarations on the liturgy after the council of Trent was penned and inserted into the Church's official document: "Sometimes in fact she admits such things into the liturgy itself, as long as they harmonize with its true and authentic spirit." With these words the Council opened the door to liturgical pluralism within the Roman rite. Its consequences are still hard to predict. Does it mean creation of new rites whose structures and euchological elements are basically those of the Roman rite, or at least inspired by it? This seems to be the mind of SC 23 which enjoins that "any new forms adopted should in some way grow organically from forms already existing." The process can perhaps be described as a tree that branches out, as a rite that develops into other different rites to form a Roman liturgical family. But it is also possible that pluralism will limit more and more the sphere of the Roman rite, especially in the third world, and eventually relegate it to a local rite, if not to a monument of the past. This was the fear voiced by a Council father who saw the danger of allowing changes derived from the cultural traditions of peoples in the liturgy because such might lead to the destruction of the Latin rite itself.[9]

The pluralism envisioned by SC 37 hinges around certain principles. The Church has no wish to impose a rigid liturgical uniformity in matters which do not involve the faith or the good of the community. It is obvious, explains the Conciliar Commission, that faith exacts an absolute unity; but the common good can require a relative uniformity even in matters which do not directly affect the faith. The unity of faith is not the sole principle to be observed when adapting the liturgy to various assemblies, regions and peoples.[10] The communion of churches, of regional communities and local assemblies, for example, will have to be taken into account. For the sake of fostering the essential unity of the Church a certain uniformity of liturgical forms may therefore be expedient. The degree of uniformity will vary according to the ecclesial conditions existing among regional and cultural groups. Geographical factors may also influence the degree of uniformity. "As far as possible," says SC 23, "notable differences between the rites used in adjacent regions are to be carefully avoided." But historical and cultural elements are often decisive factors, as for instance in the Philippines where, because of the lowland Filipino's assimilation of Roman Catholicism into his basic Malayan religiosity, an adaptation of liturgy in his case will resemble the Roman more closely than the Indian rite, however Asian in trait the latter may be.

SC 37 sets conditions for admitting into the liturgy elements from the people's traditions and cultures. One is negative: "Anything that is not indissolubly bound up with superstition and error." The other is positive: "as long as they harmonize with the liturgy's true and authentic spirit." It will take a laborious effort to define what is indissolubly bound up with superstition and error, or to make an index of forbidden customs and traditions. What one sometimes dismisses as superstitious may be in fact a manifestation of faith, unsophisticated and unpolished perhaps, but basically genuine faith nonetheless. In the case of a lot of popular religiosity it is diffi-

cult to determine where faith ends and where superstition begins. A deep sense of faith is often revealed in a number of folk
beliefs and practices that revolve around the cross or sacred
images which are identified with the persons represented.
Physical contact with sacred images amounts to a contact with
the power of the persons represented. At the root of all this
one can recognize *in germine* the Christian sacramental world-
view. Sacred signs contain the presence of God, of his grace
and power, of his love and concern for men. Obviously, the re-
semblance between one and the other does not do away with
the need for purification and critical evaluation. But neither
does the apparent presence of superstition and error justify
one to reject folk beliefs unconditionally and to decide *a priori*
that they cannot be made to harmonize with the authentic
spirit of the liturgy. Thus, liturgical adaptation is the admis-
sion into the liturgy of elements of culture and traditions,
which through the process of purification can serve as vehicles
of the liturgy for the utility or need of a particular cultural
group.

Vatican II's openness to liturgical pluralism becomes convincing in the light of its own declaration in SC 4 that "holy
Mother Church holds all lawfully acknowledged rites to be of
equal authority and dignity; that she wishes to preserve them
in the future and to foster them in every way." Diversity within the family of Latin rites is a sign of ecclesial unity. But SC
37 goes farther than this. It envisages new rites that will correspond more faithfully to the genius and culture of various
peoples and races.

SC 38–39: First Degree of Adaptation

These two articles treat of the legitimate variations within the Roman rite, "provided that the substantial unity of the
Roman rite is maintained" (SC 38). The meaning of substantial unity is nowhere explained, but its sense can be gathered
from SC 39 which speaks of adaptation "within the limits set
by the typical editions of the liturgical books." This means
that the substantial unity of the Roman rite is preserved in

the official books where the cases of adaptation by episcopal conferences are laid down. Such cases will not alter the basic structure and genius of the Roman rite, but they will provide it with more possibilities to respond to particular needs, especially in mission territories. Adaptations of this type are not limited to purely external elements, like rubrics and liturgical colors. They extend to the ordering of the rites themselves, that is to say, to the structure and the text, provided that the official books permit it. The area covers the sacraments, sacramentals, processions, liturgical language, sacred music and liturgical art (SC 39).

SC 38 enumerates the various groups to which the liturgy is to be adapted. These are the different assemblies, regions and peoples, especially in the missions. The Conciliar Commission explained that the word *praesertim* (especially) stresses the need for this type of adaptation in mission lands, but does not exclude the others.[11] Adaptation to various groups implies the possibility of legitimate variations from region to region, and, in the same region, from assembly to assembly. It is to be noted, however, that SC 23 urges against notable differences in the rites used in adjacent regions and *a fortiori* in adjacent assemblies.

A number of liturgical books published after Vatican II distinguish between *aptatio* and *accommodatio*. The former refers to the competence of Episcopal Conferences to make use of the possibilities granted by the official books. Adaptations of this type are submitted to the Holy See for confirmation. The latter, on the other hand, refers to the competence of individual ministers to adapt to particular assemblies, times and places according to the specifications of the official books, whether in the Praenotanda or in the ritual itself.

A cursory glance at the Rite of Baptism for Children can give an idea of the actual state of the matter.[12] The Introduction to Christian Initiation indicates the areas of adaptation allowed to the bishops' conferences according to the spirit of SC 38–39: the retention of local usages or their adaptation to the new rite, translations which accord more with the language and culture of the people, and insertion of alternative prayer formulas whenever the rite offers *formulas ad libitum*. The Introduction to the Rite of Baptism mentions concrete instances such as the omission of the anointing with the oil of catechumens, reformulation of the words of renunciation, omission of the anointing with the oil of chrism when there is a large number of children, retention of the "Ephphatha," and the postponement of baptism if parents are not sufficiently instructed in the faith.

It will not be superfluous to dwell at some length on two of the cases proposed by the rite. The omission of the anointing with the oil of catechumens is logical, since children are, after all, not catechumens. The rite should correspond to a real life situation and not to mere historical ambit from which the new rite has unfortunately not disentangled itself. A rite which is divorced from reality is an empty sign, a liturgy without efficaciousness. The Church does not celebrate fiction.

The possibility offered to omit the anointing with chrism for pragmatic reasons is perhaps one of the most disenchanting details in the new rite. If some liturgical signs no longer speak to people, it is because pragmatism has crippled them. The smooth flow of ceremony, its brevity and practicality are not the principal norms of adaptation, especially when it is a question of an important liturgical ingredient like the anointing with chrism. Besides being an ancient rite, it is rich in theological significance for a Church that has been reawakened to the priestly role of the laity. In the third world where infant baptisms keep pace with the giant strides of population growth, one can easily yield to the temptation to abbreviate the rite and to get to the business of pouring the water without further ceremony. Adaptation does not consist of trimming down the rite to its bare essentials, but of translating the Church's liturgical tradition into the language of the people.

These brief comments on the new rite of baptism bear out the complexity of adaptation. Several considerations come into play, and the bishops' conferences will have to approach the matter with discernment and critical evaluation, even if the matter has been outlined in the liturgical books![13]

The *accommodationes* which the minister may freely use in the course of the celebration should not be underestimated. For in effect, according to the mind of SC 38–39, these are the sole areas in which an individual minister may exercise his competence in the liturgy. *Accommodationes* are not some form of *consuelo de bobo* (consolation for the stupid) which is accepted with resentment. The proper choice of readings and prayers is crucial to any meaningful liturgical celebration, whether this be Roman, Byzantine or Indian. It is here that liturgy gets into contact with the Christian assembly. Only a pastor can feel the pulse of his community and respond to its needs. Even little details like the rubric "he addresses them in these or similar words" are significant, for they offer possibilities for a more cordial and personalized atmosphere.

With this limited number of examples one can draw for oneself a picture of the Roman rite today. No longer monolithic, it tries to satisfy the demands of a universal rite. Without sacrificing its substantial unity it tries to adjust itself to the different cultures, races and traditions. This is probably its means of survival. But one can ask whether SC 38–39 suffices to grapple with the problem of adapting the liturgy to the different conditions obtaining in the world of today, especially among peoples of different cultural backgrounds.

SC 40: Second Degree of Adaptation

The aim of this article, according to the Conciliar Commission, is to apply to the liturgy the principle of adaptation affirmed by the Popes whenever they treated of the Church's missionary activity.[14] Accordingly the proposed text stressed the missionary context of this article by expressly bringing the mission lands into focus. The need to adapt the liturgy to their culture, explains the Commission, is an urgent matter. This can be gathered from the concern shown by the Popes to adapt the Church and her liturgy to mission lands, from the indults granted to them by the Holy See, from recent developments of missionary activity in Asia and Africa, from the requests sent to the Council on behalf of these regions, and from the early Church's practice of adapting her worship to the needs and the genius of every nation.

The final text, however, has softened the missionary thrust of this article. The explicit reference to the missions was dropped at the insistence of some Council fathers who reaffirmed that the conditions found in the so-called non-missionary countries did not differ much from those in the missions.[15] This detail is significant, for it tells us that radical adaptation is not restricted to mission countries. This means that a French, German or American adaptation of the liturgy stands as equal a chance of realization as a Filipino, Indian or Zairean liturgy. It should be remembered that once upon a time in the West there were other rites besides the Roman.[16] Enamored by things Roman, Charlemagne imported the Roman rite and practically abolished the Gallican liturgy in his kingdom.[17] The Celtic liturgy began to disappear from Ireland only in the twelfth century, while the Spanish (Visigothic) liturgy prevailed until the fifteenth century in the regions dominated by the Moors. In the eighteenth century attempts were made among some French bishops to revive the Gallican liturgy. The efforts of Dom Prosper Guéranger of Solesmes in favor of the Roman rite halted a movement that could have resulted in a French liturgy.[18] Today in spite of the massive volume of cultural interchange among Western nations, one still notes a cultural pluralism among them. One can only muse whether such a pluralism coupled with the "neo-missionary" situation should not constitute grounds for liturgical adaptation in the West.[19]

SC 40 outlines the procedure for radical adaptation in three paragraphs. The first entrusts to the competent territorial ecclesiastical authority the task of determining "which elements from the traditions and genius of individual peoples might appropriately be admitted into divine worship." Findings which are judged to be useful or necessary are then to be submitted to the Holy See for its consent. The second paragraph deals with the preliminary experiments over a determined period of time among limited groups. The Holy See will

grant power to the bishops' conferences to regulate such experiments. The careful wording of this paragraph reveals the
fear, perhaps legitimate, of unjustified innovations once the
door is opened to experiments. Insatiable thirst for novelty
and impatience at the slowness of the bishops' conferences to
cope with the demands of meaningful celebrations are often
responsible for haphazard experiments. SC 40 places much of
the burden on the shoulder of Church leaders who are expected not only to support the task of adaptation, but also to take
the initiative, to lay out the plan, to lead and to direct. No law
can totally eliminate abuses, but the bishops' interest and active involvement will at least minimize them. And although
the initiative can come from the grass roots, it is ideal that it
should come from the leaders. All this, of course, requires the
technical assistance of experts, especially in mission lands
where adaptation is expected to present greater difficulties.[20]
This is the content of the third paragraph. In practice it is obvious that consultation has to extend beyond the group of liturgists. Liturgical adaptation involves theology, exegesis,
sociology, anthropology, psychology, linguistics and the arts.
Interdisciplinary consultation should be a distinctive feature
of adaptation.[21] Liturgists cannot engage in fruitful work of
adaptation all by themselves. Adaptation cannot be undertak-
en singlehandedly.

Which indigenous elements can be admitted into the liturgy? SC 40 gives a broad answer. They are "elements from
the traditions and genius of individual peoples." It is thus necessary to read this article in conjunction with SC 37 which
enumerates more specifically some of these elements: genius
(*animi ornamenta*), talents (*dotes*) and customs (*mores*). The
enumeration is not exhaustive but descriptive of what basically constitutes culture—the people's inherent genius which
finds adequate expression in different cultural ingredients,
such as values, social customs, religious rites, thought and language patterns, literature and the arts. It is obvious that for
liturgical purposes these ingredients should not be scaled
equally in usefulness or importance. And granting that they
are not indissolubly bound up with superstition and error,

they must still fulfill the conditions laid down by SC 37, namely that they harmonize with the true and authentic spirit of the liturgy, and by SC 40, that they are useful or necessary.

Some authors exclude certain natural values and non-Christian religious rituals from the list of adaptable elements on "theological" grounds.[22] According to them, values which have been surpassed by Christianity, like élan vital, fertility, fatherhood and motherhood, may not be admitted into the liturgy without their first undergoing the process of Christianization. By the process of Christianization is meant a radical reorientation of these values to the Christian mystery, in such a way that fertility, for instance, would refer exclusively to the fecundity of Christ's mediatorship, while élan vital would refer to divine life. One cannot but nurture misgivings about such a method of spiritualization. For while Christianity may exhibit qualities surpassing the purely natural it does not annihilate or render human values inefficacious. Indeed SC 37 declares that the Church preserves them intact. Furthermore, to impair the vigor of natural values amounts to the weakening of sacramental symbolism which necessarily invokes them. To transpose the natural to the supernatural, fertility to Christ's mediatorship, élan vital to divine life, human fatherhood to divine fatherhood, and human motherhood to the motherhood of the Church is to confuse the issue and empty human values of their intrinsic worth. The right attitude of a Christian, even in the liturgy, is to acknowledge the natural gifts of God, to bless and thank him for them, and to pray that through them he may partake of God's eternal gifts. Christianization does not consist so much of spiritualizing natural values as of imbuing the person with Christian values. Our forebears held this view of things and meant it when they spoke of the fertility of women and soil as God's benevolence, of their offspring as God's gifts, and of their daily food as grace. These blessings they celebrated with abandon in dances before the Lord and his saints or in processions for which they decked streets and houses with first fruits.[23]

The objection against non-Christian rituals is understandable in the face of the Church's traditional reluctance to adapt them in her worship. The Chinese Rites controversy which beset the Church for over a hundred years typifies her attitude of extreme reserve toward paganism.[24] The question is a delicate one and should not be handled in a simplistic and puritanical fashion by dismissing all non-Christian rituals as erroneous and superstitious, or as having been abolished by the new law.[25] Obviously the non-Christian should not be confused with the Christian, but neither should the former be identified with error, unless by error we mean the lack of fullness of truth. Vatican II's Decree on the Missionary Activity of the Church (AG) gives a profound theological insight into the matter. AG 9 not only insinuates that there is truth and grace to be found among the nations, as a sort of secret presence of God, but also declares that "whatever good is found to be sown in the hearts and minds of men, or in the rites and cultures peculiar to various peoples, is not lost. More than that, it is healed, ennobled, and perfected for the glory of God, the shame of the demon, and the bliss of men." In many ways liturgical adaptation tends toward eschatological fullness when the divine endowments to the nations shall have been recapitulated in Christ. It should be noted that SC 37–40, which is an earlier document, does not dichotomize the purely cultural and the purely religious. Religious rituals are an essential ingredient of every culture. The Indian culture cannot be conceived of without its temples and religious celebrations. But the situation varies even regionally in a country; thus, for example, the adaptation of pagan rituals in the liturgy is of no special interest to lowland Filipinos, unless one wishes to confront the problem of the vestiges of paganism which one detects in such clandestine practices as killing a chicken and pouring its blood on the foundations of a house, as still happens even in a city like Manila.[26] However, for missionaries who work among the so-called "cultural minority groups" in the third world, the question is urgent. Authors who exclude pagan religious rituals from the list of adaptable elements mention bloody sacrifices and circumcision on grounds that these have been abolished by the New Testament. They will allow a compromise, if the rites are part and parcel of social life or have shed all their religious undertones. Even then, however, they can only be incorporated in the extra-liturgical activity of the community after they have been duly purified of error and superstition. This rigorous opinion seems to be a carryover of Propaganda Fide's instruction *Plane Compertum* of 1939 which reopened the Chinese Rites controversy and permitted participation in the rites, because in the course of time, the instruction declares, they have become a purely civil or social affair.[27]

It is not the scope of this book to enter into such details as bloody sacrifices and circumcision. It cannot be gathered from the New Testament writings that circumcision has been abolished or forbidden as a *religious ritual*. What appears is that the apostles no longer imposed it on the Gentiles as a condition for becoming Christians.[28] Bloody sacrifices, on the other hand, pose some real theological difficulties because of the unique and infinite efficacy of Christ's sacrifice on the cross.[29] Although Acts 21:26 seems to suggest that Paul took part in the temple sacrifice, and although some early Quartodecimanian communities apparently celebrated Easter according to the Jewish ritual (with or without the paschal lamb?), one cannot rely on conjectural information to prove that the early Church offered bloody sacrifices. This is not to say that bloody sacrifices are altogether unknown in Christian tradition. The Ritual of the Armenian Church has, in fact, a canon on the sacrifice of a yearling animal before the door of the church in the presence of a priest.[30] The prayer underlines the essential character of the act as reparation for sins, fulfillment of a vow, or petition for divine blessing on flocks and the fields. It is not easy to evaluate the theological import of this rite which, at any rate, has no significant bearing on other Christian churches. One can probably interpret it as the faithful's sign of recognition of God's sovereignty. It should really not contradict or throw any doubt on the uniqueness of Christ's sacrifice, if it is performed with the awareness that it has value only in view of the cross, and that it is one's symbol of external manifestation of joining in the eternal sacrifice of Christ. In this sense one can speak also of the sacrifice of incense and the offering of the fruits of the earth. To strike a correct theological balance, it is necessary to add that all this should not question the sufficiency of the sacramental system, but rather fill up its cultural gap. Thus for a "non-verbal" society where gestures speak louder than words, or gestures are themselves the words,[31] such rites can perhaps take the liturgical dimension of Amen, of a response of "yes" to the offer of salvation, of participation in the mystery of Christ. Needless to say, the problem is more intricate than one may suspect. One can easily go off the deep end in the name of adaptation. But it can be equally disastrous to ignore the issue completely, even on the level of theoretical possibility, in the name of prudence.

How has the post-conciliar Church met the vision of SC 40? The Introduction to Christian Initiation exhorts the bishops' conferences to examine possible elements from the traditions and cultures of different peoples which can be admitted into the liturgy of baptism, and to submit them to the Holy See for its consent.[32] This provision which echoes SC 40 applies to the mission as well as to the non-mission territories. The provision, however, which is taken from SC 65, deals more explicitly on missionary situations where more possibilities for an indigenous baptismal rite are offered.[33] Once again it is left to the bishops' conferences to discern those elements from indigenous initiation rites which can be adapted. Rites of initiation to the tribe, to maturity or to social responsibility are never lacking in any society. Investigation and critical evaluation of these rites can yield impressive results that can deepen the people's understanding of baptism. When one considers the wealth of every people's traditions and what these have to offer to Christ and his Church, one sees a bright future with a plentiful harvest of the Spirit.

III
The Theological Principle of Adaptation

It has been said that what we need in the third world is not so much liturgical adaptation as a good translation of texts and better music. This is not the place to engage in polemics nor is there any need to make an issue of it. One who reads the signs of the times will not even debate on the prudence of sailing with the current. In Asia it may be the only way to survive and be relevant. The disastrous Chinese Rites controversy has taught the Church in Asia that "unbending soldiers get no victories." When the signs of the times indicate that a country wishes to preserve its family and national traditions or to return to them, the Church will do well to follow in the same train or else face the embarrassment of an overstaying alien. In matters which are not essential to the Gospel the Church can learn from the wisdom of a Chinese aphorism: "The stiffest tree is readiest for the axe; the strong and mighty topple from their place; the soft and yielding rise above them all."[1]

But expedience is not the sole nor the principal reason for adaptation. The main reason must be sought in the nature the Church as the prolongation in time and space of the incarnation of the Word of God.[2] In the final analysis, the mystery of the incarnation is the theological principle of adaptation. The Word of God, in assuming the condition of man, except sin, bound himself to the history, culture, traditions and religion of his own people. The Word was made flesh, that is to say, he became a Jew, a member of the chosen people. In the words of St. Paul, "From their flesh and blood came Christ who is above all, God for ever blessed" (Rom. 9:5). More pointedly he writes, "When the appointed time came, God sent his Son, born of a woman, born subject to the law" (Gal. 4:4). The Word of God, in other words, assumed not only what pertained to the human race, but also what was proper to the Jewish race. He inherited its natural traits, its genius, its spiritual endowments and its peculiar mode of self-expression. He was a Jew in every way, except in sin. The historicity of the incarnation demanded that he identify himself with his own people in heart and mind, in flesh and blood.

Far from limiting the sphere of the incarnation, such a vision guarantees the universality of Christ and his Gospel. The fact that the Word became a Jew gives us the assurance that in his resurrected state he can, even today, incarnate himself in different races and cultures through the faith of the Church and the celebration of his mystery. Because he identified himself with the people of Israel to whom God entrusted the promise of salvation, the incarnate Word can identify himself with the rest of humanity whom God called to take part in the promise made to Abraham.[3] The Christ of faith is the universal Christ, the man for others, because he was an historical Christ.

The once-for-all character of the incarnation is the key to the understanding of the Church's role in the work of salvation.[4] Through the Church, the non-repeatable historical event becomes actual, and Christ continues to be actively present in the world. The extent of the Church's incarnation in various races and cultures will be the extent of Christ's universality. The incarnation is an historical event, but its mystery lives on whenever the Church assumes the social and cultural conditions of the people among whom she dwells. Adaptation is thus not an option, but a theological imperative arising from incarnational exigency. The Church must incarnate herself in every race, as Christ incarnated himself in the Jewish race. AG 10 declares that "the Church must become part of all these groups for the same motive which led Christ to bind himself, in virtue of his incarnation, to the definite social and cultural conditions of those human beings among whom he dwelt."[5] The procedure proposed by the Council is one of integration, after the example of Christ who "entangled" himself with a particular people. This means that the Church cannot remain a stranger to the people with whom she lives; she must be adopted by it. This pluralistic view will not hurt the universality of the Church; on the contrary, it will foster it. For there can be no truly universal Church without truly local churches. These, says AG 22, will have their own place in the ecclesial communion only if they adorn themselves with their own traditions and define their own identity as local churches. Underlying this statement is the Council's vision of catholic unity, borrowed and adopted from patristic theology, which speaks of the recapitulation of all things in Christ.[6] In the significant words of AG 22, "Particular traditions, together with the individual patrimony of each family of nations, can be illumined by the light of the Gospel, and then be taken up into Catholic unity."

Incarnation brings about mutual enrichment to the people who receive the faith and to the Church who incarnates herself. The local churches (AG 22 focuses its attention on "young churches") must imitate the plan of the incarnation of the Word of God, so that, rooted in Christ and built upon the foundation of the apostles, they may "take to themselves in a wonderful exchange all the riches of the nations which were given to Christ as an inheritance." The *admirabile commercium* of the incarnation, whereby the Creator of the human race took to himself the nature of man and enriched it with the gift of divine nature, is the model that the Council proposes to the young churches.[7] With deep respect the Council acknowledges the presence of God in the cultures and endowments of various nations and encourages the churches to adorn themselves with the traditions of their people, with their wisdom and learning, with their arts and sciences, unto the glory of the Creator, the revelation of the Savior's grace and the proper arrangement of Christian life. In gathering together the scattered fruits of the Word sown among the peoples, the Church brings about by the power of the Spirit the eschatological fullness when God will be all in all. At the same time, the riches of the nations, illumined by the Gospel, receive from the fullness of Christ. By this wondrous exchange cultures and traditions are made all the richer.

The task of adaptation of the Church in Asia was given a fresh impetus and a sense of urgency by a letter of Paul VI to Asian bishops: "The propagation of the Christian message must in no way cancel out or lessen these cultural and spiritual values, which constitute a priceless heritage. The Church must make herself in her fullest expression native to your countries, your cultures, your races. . . . Let the Church draw nourishment from the genuine values of venerable Asian religions and cultures."[8] The letter is not a novelty in the area of adaptation. At most it is a timely application of the principles formulated by Vatican II or an echo of the 1659 instruction of Propaganda Fide to the Vicars Apostolic of China.[9] It is a clarion voice rousing the Asians to assume the task of adaptation. Asia has so much to offer to Christ and his Church. Its ancient cultures tested by the vicissitudes of time, its sacred traditions heavy with age and buttressed on the bedrock of Asian genius, its social refinements equaled only by the splendor of its religious rituals: from all these the Church can draw nourishment. These she must claim for Christ for whom they yearn and in whom they find their fullness.

The exchange between Christian cult and native culture involves certain adjustments in both. Cultural ingredients will have to pass through the death of purification and critical evaluation. They will have to shed off every claim to finality and assume their proper role as God's prophetic instruments for the revelation of Jesus Christ. When Christians adapted Jewish rituals to their worship, they regarded them as types and prophecies of Christian realities, as shadows of Christian truth. Thus Justin Martyr gives the generic title of "prophet" to Old Testament readings at the liturgy of the Word.[10] And the Mass of the Roman rite regards them as prophetic preparations for the New Testament. In its traditional scheme of readings it called the Old Testament *propheta*.[11] This practice indicates the attitude of the Church when she adapts indigenous elements into the liturgy. Christian revelation holds primacy over every human creation. Everything must tend toward it. In practice this can be as simple as finding an indigenous element which can illustrate the message of the liturgy, or it can be as complex and delicate as introducing the reading of the sacred books of non-Christian religions in the liturgy. While the Church in the Philippines might not be confronted by the latter case, in India, which possesses sacred scriptures, the Church is put to the test.[12] To accept them she must conjure up solid theological reasons which satisfy the requirement of faith; to reject them she must be willing to face the consequence of further alienation from the Hindu world.

But contact with indigenous culture implies certain accommodations also on the part of the Christian liturgy. The history of the Roman rite during its migration to the Franco-Germanic regions is an example of how culture irresistibly modifies what it receives.[13] And perhaps this is the best thing that can happen to the liturgy, if it is to become native to every culture. And since no culture is static, the liturgy will be constantly subjected to modifications. In this sense the incarnation of the Church's worship will be an on-going process. While its basic content must remain unvaried, its structure, language and symbols will have to bear the mark of each culture. In one culture it may mean adaptation according to SC 38–39; in another it may mean a radical restructuring of forms, creation of new texts[14] and the use of native signs.

Liturgical pluralism is an incarnational imperative, rather than a concession of Vatican II.[15] The Church must prolong the incarnation of Christ in time and space. This she can realize only through the faith which she proclaims and celebrates. In other words, her liturgy must be embedded on the culture and traditions of the people. Liturgical pluralism is a necessary corollary to the premise of the Church's obligation to be local and native. Where the Church has become indigenous, where the hierarchy and laity come from the ranks of the people, there her liturgy will have to be native. A borrowed rite is an alien rite. There should be no dichotomy between the liturgy and the life of a native Church.

IV
The Liturgical Principle of Adaptation

Liturgical adaptation rests on principles derived from the nature of the liturgy itself. Even after the requirements of orthodoxy and culture have been met, certain conditions set down by the liturgy have to be observed. It is not correct to say that the purity of faith is all that matters, or that the gauge of adaptation is the cultural element alone. Christian liturgy has its own imperatives. Some of these are obvious from the nature of the liturgy itself, while others can be derived from the tradition of the Church. Comparative liturgy and history have much to offer,[1] as do the encyclical *Mediator Dei* of Pope Pius XII and the documents of Vatican II, especially the Constitution on the Sacred Liturgy.

One principle which is quite obvious is that "the liturgy is above all things the worship of the divine Majesty" (SC 33). It is the vertical line reaching from man to God.[2] It is man's personal encounter with God in faith, hope and love through Christ in the community of the Church. It is the very act of worship rendered on the cross to the Father by Christ, the high priest, an act now present in mystery in the Church.[3] The liturgy is the prayer of the total Christ, head and members.[4] This aspect of worship is so essential to the liturgy that its absence will reduce the celebration to an empty ritual. A liturgy which does not offer the possibility of a personal encounter with God lacks a basic quality. Indeed one can ask whether there is liturgy here at all. The problem often stems from a too horizontal interpretation of the word "celebration."[5] In some instances this has taken a thoroughly interpersonal dimension to the detriment of the element of prayer.[6] Prolonged group sharing of insights, exaggerated stress on the human and social relevance of the celebration, and an attitude of nonchalance, which often borders on casualness and banality—all conspire to make the liturgy nothing more than a pleasant (or unpleasant) encounter among celebrating individuals. There must be interaction, and the celebration must take the human situation into account, but not at the expense of the worship of God, of a personal encounter with him, of sharing in the Christian mystery, which the celebration unfolds and makes present. It is not a question of merely keeping a balance between worship and celebration; it is a question of priority. The reason why the Christian community gathers is in order to worship God. Celebration is the form whereby the community is able to realize this. Paschal joy and social awareness characterized the meetings of the apostolic community. These qualities did not subtract anything from the principal motive of the assembly, the praise of God. For the Church is essentially a worshiping community, "a chosen race, a royal priesthood, a consecrated nation, a people set apart to sing the praises of God" (1 Pet. 2:9). It is her vocation to proclaim the greatness of God, to worship him and, by this act of worship, to manifest herself to the world as the community of the redeemed. The liturgy must always maintain its fundamental trait of the vertical line reaching up to God, regardless of its external form or the cultural ambit to which it corresponds.

But the prayer element in the liturgy should not exclude the educative or catechetical value present in every liturgical celebration.[7] "It contains abundant instruction for the faithful. For in the liturgy God speaks to his people and Christ is still proclaiming his Gospel" (SC 33). Vatican II's directive that the liturgy should be distinguished by simplicity, brevity and clarity and that it should be within the people's power of comprehension is aimed at enhancing the catechetical value of Christian worship. The scriptural readings, the homily and the prayers, especially the eucharistic prayer, are the primary sources of instruction in the faith.[8] The Church has always jealously guarded her liturgical texts, for they are the authentic formulations of her *theologia prima*. The liturgy is her official proclamation of the faith; it is her *credo*. This explains why the prayers she uses do not bear the names of the authors, for they now belong to her. Because of its official character the liturgy cannot be used as a forum for private theological persuasions.

But the efficacy of liturgical catechesis presupposes instruction outside the celebration itself.[9] Proper disposition on the part of the faithful implies a certain amount of familiarity with the nature and structure of the liturgy, the Word of God and the prayer texts. Although the liturgy is catechetical in nature, it remains primarily an act of worship. In other words, instruction takes place in the context of prayer, not of a classroom. Liturgy is not intended for the uninitiated, but for those who, having embraced the faith and meditated on it, wish to proclaim it in the Christian assembly.[10] Liturgical catechesis is not for unbelievers or for those who will hear the Christian message for the first time.[11] As SC 33 remarks, through the reading of the Word and the Church's prayers, songs and rituals, "the faith of those taking part is nourished and their minds are raised to God, so that they may offer him the worship which reason requires and more copiously receive his grace."

Questions have been raised regarding the openness of the liturgy to the theological, social and political climate existing in particular churches.[12] Should not the liturgy, for example, use the language of liberation, in order to impress on the people the urgency of social and political reforms? Thus some experimenters incorporate liberation skits in the Mass as a form of liberation catechesis. It is obvious that a good liturgy has to reflect the experience of the community, or, to use a current expression, it must be relevant. Relevance, however, should be subjected to certain conditions. The liturgy is not a forum for the propagation of the social and political ideologies, however Christian these may be in orientation. Indeed, it is only after the community has been imbued with them that the liturgy can admit them as elements of prayer. A "liberation liturgy" can only mean that the people's aspiration for liberation has been assumed by the Church into the realm of worship. Although such a liturgy will be influenced by the ideology and language of the movement, it will have to be rooted in the Word of God and centered on the Christian mystery. The apostolic community's prayer under the persecution by the Sanhedrin, Acts 4:24–30, is a model of Christian worship in adverse situations. The community interpreted their trial in the light of God's Word, while they focused their attention on Christ and his message of salvation.

The center of every liturgical celebration is the person of Christ and his pervading paschal mystery.[13] This principle is the determining element in the definition of the Christian liturgy.[14] Whether the Church celebrates baptism or the Eucharist or prays the liturgy of the hours, she continually proclaims Christ and his paschal mystery. It is Christ's mystery that her liturgical year unfolds and makes present in mystery.[15] Even on Christmas day the Church focuses her attention on Christ's death and resurrection, the climax of the mystery of the incarnation.[16] On the feasts of saints she "proclaims the paschal mystery as achieved in the saints who have suffered and been glorified with Christ" (SC 104). Emphasis on one or another aspect of Christ's saving deed should not create the impression that the Church does not always celebrate the paschal mystery. The liturgy of Good Friday does not hide the joy of Easter from sight;[17] both the death and resurrection of Christ are celebrated on Good Friday and Easter Sunday, although with different stress and in different moods.[18]

In societies whose orientation is strongly anthropological, humanistic or secular, the liturgy will be colored by corresponding values and attitudes toward life. But the heart of the celebration will always be the Christian mystery. The liturgy does not celebrate man or life or death. The expression, "The liturgy is the celebration of life," means that the paschal mystery is celebrated in the context of the people's concrete experience. In societies like Latin America and the Philippines where popular piety and devotions are an important element of religious culture, the liturgy will use forms inspired by or borrowed from popular religious expressions in order to bring the paschal mystery closer to the experience of worshipers.[19]

Christocentric orientation is to be understood in the framework of salvation history and the process of man's encounter with God. *Ad Patrem per Filium in Spiritu Sancto:* to the Father, through the Son, in the Holy Spirit.[20] The Father, to whom theology attributes the work of creation, is the source and finality of human life, and consequently of human worship. The original Christian liturgy addressed its prayers to the Father. To the Son, on the other hand, is attributed the work of redemption. He is the great Liturgist and the one and only Mediator between God and man. In the liturgy the Church approaches the Father through the mediatorship of Christ. Stated another way, Christ is the true worshiper of the Father; he represents the Church before the throne of grace.[21] The conclusion of liturgical prayers, "through Christ our Lord," expresses the process of encounter between God and man. Finally, to the Holy Spirit theology attributes the work of sanctification. By his power the redemptive act of Christ is actualized and made present in mystery. Just as the incarnation of the Word of God in the womb of Mary was realized through his intervention, so the rebirth of God's people in the womb of the Church is brought about by his power. It is he who consecrates the bread and the wine on the altar and sets men apart for the ministry of the Church.[22] Thus we go to the Father through Christ "in the unity of the Holy Spirit." In the liturgy man does not worship without the Spirit.[23] Indeed, it is the Spirit that prays within him.[24]

Another basic principle of liturgical adaptation is the primacy of God's written Word.[25] "Sacred Scripture is of paramount importance in the celebration of the liturgy," says SC 24. Liturgical adaptation has always maintained this principle.[26] Readings are taken from Scripture, and the homily, prayers and symbols draw inspiration from it. It is not an exaggeration to say that the Word of God is sacramental; it effects what it says. Through it God speaks to his people and Christ proclaims his Gospel. Its acceptance in faith sanctifies man. All this explains the deep respect given by the liturgy to the Holy Bible. The external signs of veneration shown to it express the Church's firm conviction that here one is dealing with the very Word of God himself. Unfortunately the importance of the Word is all too often neglected because non-biblical literature has taken the place reserved to biblical readings or because liturgical gimmicks[27] draw the people's attention away from God's Word.

Active participation is another basic principle of liturgical adaptation. It is one of the happy "rediscoveries" of Vatican II, whose values cannot be overestimated. Much has been written on the subject and there is no need to repeat all the details here.[28] SC 14 declares that full, conscious and active participation in the liturgy is demanded by the very nature of the liturgy and is the right and duty of the Christian people by reason of their baptism. Therefore, "in the restoration and promotion of the sacred liturgy, this full and active participation by all the people is the aim to be considered before all else." This explains SC's insistence on liturgical catechesis and the need to reform liturgical rites. The attempt to recapture the spirit and character of the Roman rite of the fifth and seventh century can be explained in this light.[29] SC 34 exhorts that "the rites should be distinguished by a noble simplicity; they should be short, clear, and unencumbered by useless repetitions." Intelligent participation requires a certain transparency of the rites. In many ways the liturgical reform of Vatican II has succeeded in bringing the Roman rite back to its pristine simplicity and clarity. But it can be asked if such typical Roman qualities are equally valued by all. To a colorful and exuberant people the simplicity of the Roman rite will appear cold and anemic; the conciseness of its liturgical texts will strike them as flat and their directness as blunt. Even brevity does not enjoy the same degree of desirability in every culture. The pace of life and religious culture are factors which will determine the length of the liturgical action. And one should add here that intelligibility is a quality which does not have to remove the sense of mystery from the celebration. In other words, the simplicity of the reformed Roman liturgy has a relative value and does not always and everywhere guarantee full, conscious and active participation.

What is the extent of the people's participation in the liturgy? SC 28 offers a general norm: "In liturgical celebrations, whether as a minister or as one of the faithful, each person should perform his role by doing solely and totally what the nature of things and liturgical norms require of him." This is a principle based on the hierarchical nature of the liturgy which St. Ignatius of Antioch advocated in his letters[30] and SC 41–42 has confirmed. Each person has his specific role to perform in the liturgy. The order of the community demands that no one should desert his duty or usurp another's. Thus the recitation of the entire eucharistic prayer in unison by priest and assembly is a misrepresentation of active participation, because the eucharistic prayer is a presidential prayer. On the other hand, a one-man show by the priest, who reads all the lessons, conducts the choir and leads the assembly while he performs his role at the altar as president, indicates that the community is not ready for liturgical celebration. The different roles and ministries in the Roman rite need not be discussed here. It should be noted, however, that the present-day delineation of liturgical roles is the product of historical evolution. The homily and eucharistic prayer, which were originally reserved to the bishop as his "special liturgy," were gradually taken over by presbyters, while the Lord's Prayer, which was traditionally a presidential prayer in the Roman Mass,[31] is now recited or sung by both the president and the assembly. New pastoral exigencies and theological trends are valid factors for the reassessment of liturgical roles and ministries. We may not close the door to a lesser or greater participation on the basis of historical fixity. But the door stays closed on acephalous celebrations which ignore the distinction between the role of the president and that of the assembly.[32]

The question of liturgical signs will always engage the interest of persons dedicated to the work of adaptation in the Church.[33] Of tremendous bearing on the subject is the principle enunciated by SC 21: "The liturgy is made up of unchangeable elements divinely instituted, and elements subject to change." Some liturgical signs claim divine authorship (water for baptism, food and drink for the Eucharist), while others cite an ecclesiastical origin. The latter, says SC 21, "not only may but ought to be changed with the passing of time if features have by chance crept in which are less harmonious with the intimate nature of the liturgy, or if existing elements have grown less functional." Signs which no longer convey the message of the liturgy nor speak to the people are empty, lack efficacy and betray the very purpose of liturgical signs. One is perhaps tempted to conclude that they must therefore be changed. But such a conclusion without further qualification is open to debate. For there are signs which may not be understood, because they happen to belong to another cultural milieu or have been obscured by historical evolution. It seems that the right approach to the matter is catechesis, which situates liturgical signs in their cultural and historical context. Immersion-bath as a sign of initiation may not be universally practiced, but it can be understood in the perspective of the biblical world. The eloquence of the rite of commingling in the Roman Mass has been muted by mystical interpretations, but an historical explanation can redeem its significance.[34] In other words, one may not discard traditional signs simply because they are no longer understood by the people. One of the aims of liturgical instruction is precisely to bridge the gap between culture and history. Liturgical adaptation does not find its justification in the fact that the traditional Greco-Roman and Franco-Germanic signs are incomprehensible to the third world, but rather on the fact that these signs are alien to the cultural expressions of the third world.

In every sign one can distinguish the exterior form from the reality or content which it signifies. In dealing with liturgical signs it is useful to keep in mind that the exterior form has been conditioned by culture, biblical and non-biblical, while the content has been determined by Christ himself (in the case of the sacraments) or by the Church through her laws and traditions. Furthermore, between the form and the content there is often a relationship based on connaturality, that is to say, the form possesses a natural quality or characteristic, which enables it to signify the reality intended by Christ and the Church. Lastly, with respect to the content, the will of Christ and the liturgical tradition of the Church, insofar as this involves the faith, demand an absolute fidelity. With respect, however, to exterior forms one must distinguish between those elements which are essential to the definition of the rite itself and those which are contingent on the cultural milieu and are consequently not indispensable to the essence of the rite. Baptism, which is a washing in water, can be signified only by water. On the other hand, bread and wine, or more specifically wheat bread and grape wine, are dependent on the agriculture of the place and the eating habits of the people. Although bread and wine are of biblical provenance and deserve special respect because of their association with the history of salvation, they are bound with culture and can be substituted with equivalent signs found in other cultures. Needless to say, the supreme authority of the Church, the theological climate which obtains in local churches and the socio-religious response of the people have a decisive role in the matter. What is theoretically admissible is not always pastorally expedient.

Time and again the question of using native food and beverage for the Eucharist has been raised in regions where wheat and grapes are not grown and importation has become difficult. The use of wine becomes even more problematic in Buddhist countries where devout Buddhists take offense at the public drinking of alcoholic beverages. Religious culture has branded wine as a thing of vice, and the Christian cup of salvation has become a cup of malice. May the Church impose her religious culture on them by insisting on the use of the wine and defending its innocence?

One of the usual arguments brought forward in favor of native eucharistic elements is hypothetical: If Christ had instituted the Eucharist in the third world, he would have chosen native food and drink. Certainly the principle of the incarnation would have "constrained" him to do so, as it did in Palestine. But the argument remains a hypothetical one with little or no value. A more valid argument is of ecclesial type: the duty of the Church to adapt herself to various cultures *ad instar oeconomiae incarnationis.* How can she realize this in the case of the Eucharist? One approach is to determine the motive of Christ for his choice of bread and wine. According to Joachim Jeremias, "Jesus made the broken bread a simile of the fate of his body, the blood of the grapes a simile of his outpoured blood."[35] Thus when substituting bread and wine with native elements, one has to take into account the latter's connaturality to signify the violent death of Jesus on the cross. The name, "breaking of bread," given by the early Christians to the Eucharist suggests that the Last Supper of Jesus had a sacrificial overtone. The gesture of breaking the bread possesses a deep theological significance and should not be left out in the process of substitution. The kind of cereal or foodstuff will depend on the crops produced in the region. There is no clear biblical indication that the eucharistic bread must be made of wheat. John 6:13, a eucharistic pericope,[36] speaks of barley loaves. And it does not seem essential to the veracity of the sacramental sign that the drink should be inebriating. Christ must have chosen wine, not because it is inebriating, but because it is the biblical symbol of blood.

But the depth of liturgical adaptation is measured, not by external signs, even on the sacramental level, but by the use of a language that reflects the thought of the people.[37] The use of native symbols and motifs can help to create an indigenous atmosphere and bring out the transparency of liturgical signs, but the real test is the kind of language that the liturgy employs. As long as the Church prays and speaks in a foreign language whose pattern of thought and mode of expression is alien to the people, all efforts at adaptation remain superficial. This means that the Church has not penetrated the realm of the spirit nor fully appreciated the native genius of the people. Language is an authentic manifestation of the way people form ideas and interiorly react to objective reality. Language communicates the soul and spirit of the people and betrays their most secret sentiments.

However, we are not dealing here with awkward but faithful translations of liturgical texts. Translations will often be either beautiful but unfaithful to the original, or faithful but ugly and irrelevant. The insufficiency of translation is now accepted as a matter of fact, especially in non-Western countries. The use of the vernacular has made the liturgy intelligible but not closer to the heart of the people. Beneath every translation is a message originally communicated to another people.[38] A translation, even in paraphrase form, cannot adequately transmit this message to the people of this age and culture without breaking away from its original mode of expression. Adaptation necessarily implies the composition of new liturgical texts.[39] Anything less than this falls short of the goal of SC 37 and 40.

The composition of new liturgical texts should not be taken to mean *creatio ex nihilo*. Liturgical creativity draws inspiration from existing rites. This was the procedure that the Church observed during the fourth century, when her liturgical creativity was at its best. Official texts should serve as immediate sources, for it is here that the Church transmits the apostolic tradition and the original meaning of her rituals. Adaptation means conveying these things according to the thought and language pattern of the people. This is not a betrayal of tradition; it is the sowing of the seed of divine revelation on native soil where it will eventually take root and grow according to existing natural conditions. This will often involve the use of linguistic patterns like idiomatic expressions and paraphrases of proverbs and maxims. For these are cultural elements that capture the spirit and genius of the people. Through them the people are able to identify a reality as their own and claim it as part and parcel of their life.

It becomes clear that liturgical texts will have to be composed, not in Latin or the vernacular, but in the mother tongue of the people. The fact that English is understood and spoken by many citizens of the third world countries does not make it an adequate liturgical language for those peoples. The insertion of geographical and historical details in the English prayer, originally conceived and formulated in English, may add some nationalistic flavor but will not qualify it as an indigenous prayer. Adaptation is not equivalent to a national-ism which seeks parallels between the history of salvation and the history of a nation, or between the heroes of faith and political patriots. It does not, of course, exclude the possibility of situating national events and personages in the context of God's saving plan. But the main thrust of adaptation is to reformulate the one mystery of faith proclaimed and celebrated by the Church throughout the world in the language that fully and faithfully reflects the spirit, the genius and the sensitivity and aspirations of the people.

It is not always easy to determine the kind of language to be used in the liturgy.[40] In general one can affirm that it should not come straight from the streets and marketplaces. Banality and vulgarity in the liturgy are absolutely offensive, not to say detestable. Liturgical language must be noble and prayerful, as befits the dignity and solemnity of the community's act of worship. One should add that it should be simple. Simplicity means that words and expressions are intelligible to the majority of the worshiping assembly.[41] It does not exclude the occasional use of poetic forms, especially in solemn liturgical celebrations. It should not be archaic or esoteric. Such a language will defeat the purpose of liturgical communication. The evolution of a language should also be taken into account. Idiomatic expressions and colloquial usages vary from region to region and will have to be adjusted accordingly. In the final analysis, the spontaneous reaction of the people is the best measure to gauge the success of adaptation.

V

The Cultural Principle
of Adaptation

From the historical background of SC 37–40 a significant
fact has emerged. Adaptation is not primarily a missionary
concern but a cultural exigency. The motive is not merely to
facilitate the activity of the Church in mission lands, but to
make the liturgy available and relevant to every culture. Indeed, Vatican II's liturgical reform was premised on the need
"to meet the circumstances and needs of modern times," as
SC 4 has declared. Obviously, the third world countries have
been the immediate beneficiaries of the Council's openness to
liturgical pluralism, as one can gather from the special indults
and privileges granted to them after the Council. But the display of good will is not exactly on account of their being mission lands but because of their strikingly distinct cultures.
That is why the recent efforts at liturgical adaptation in India,
Zaire and the Philippines are all markedly cultural in their
features. It is thus unfair to restrict the zone of adaptation to
the third world, as if Western countries did not experience the
urgency to adapt the Roman liturgy to their cultures.[1]

Culture may be viewed from various angles and defined
accordingly. For our purpose it is enough to describe it in general terms as the sum total of human values, of social and religious traditions and rituals, and of the modes of expression
through language and the arts, all of which are rooted in the
particular genius of the people.[2] By genius is meant the natural thought and language pattern, the spontaneous mode of re-

acting interiorly to reality, and the manner in which the intellectual, emotional and effective sensitivity is exteriorized. To appreciate a culture it is not enough to be impressed by its monuments, rituals and the complexity of language. One has to take into consideration the people's genius which underlies all these exterior expressions.[3] Therefore, to define any culture, it is necessary to frame it in the context of the genius that gave birth to it. One can discuss what this genius consists of, but perhaps by way of example mention can be made of the Filipino ability to synthesize diverse, even conflicting, cultural ingredients with his native values and traditions,[4] so that anything foreign he touches undergoes a cultural metamorphosis. Lowland Filipino music, dances and architecture, for example, are a fascinating synthesis of East and West, of old and new.[5] If culture is approached from the angle of the genius that created it, the question regarding the colonial origin of some of Filipino values and rituals becomes tangential. Defining Filipino culture involves searching not only for native traditions that antedate colonialism, but also for the result of four hundred years of cultural assimilation and synthesis.

Every culture is in constant evolution. This phenomenon becomes especially problematic in countries that are caught in the process of rapid transition from agriculture to industrialization and urbanization.[6] Rational reflection is often unable to keep pace with the corresponding changes in world-view, outlook on life and attitude toward religion and the Church. By and large, one notes the ebbing away of attachment to traditional values and rituals. To protect indigenous culture from total extinction, the State in many countries has instituted positive measures, such as museums and folk-art presentations. But such efforts are in fact indicative of the decline of an indigenous culture's active influence upon the daily life of the people, particularly in urban settlements. Decline here is not equivalent to fossilization. No traditional cultural form vanishes completely from the consciousness or the subconscious of the society which it nurtured over generations and on which it imprinted a particular character. That is why museum pieces are not utterly alien to the daily life of a nation.

A question has been raised on the phase of culture which is best suited for adaptation. Should traditional forms be discarded in favor of modern ones? AG 21 suggests that indigenous culture be developed "in accordance with modern conditions" and finally be perfected in Christ. In this sense someone has remarked that adaptation does not mean "adapting to a fossilized culture, but a daring entrance into the building up of a new world, bringing along to its construction valuable Christian elements."[7] In reality the matter has more loose ends than one may suspect. In the Asian context, for instance, there is a strong temptation to regard ancient traditions as irrelevant, if not hindrances to modern progress, which is unfortunately identified only with Western civilization. This is an alarming and lamentable realization that dawns on one who reads the objection made by an Indian to the Indian Mass: "What is the fun of adapting ourselves to ancient Indian culture and religious forms while India is going modern and Western, throwing overboard her traditional culture and religious practices? Most educated non-Christians are taking to Western ways. Indianization is going backward while India wants to march ahead."[8] Such an objection betrays a misconception of native culture as something static, self-enclosed and unable to open itself to foreign influences. Culture is self-rejuvenating. The version of modernization, which suppresses traditional culture, causes irreparable damage to the people's native genius and to its racial and cultural identity. In the Philippines this is the genius we see at work. It assimilates foreign elements and synthesizes them with the traditional culture. The question should be answered in the context of cultural evolution. Adaptation does not mean returning to primitive or discarded ways. But neither does it mean futuristic approach or assumption of cultural forms that are still in the process of being assimilated. Adaptation refers to firmly established values and traditions which have shaped for many generations the religious, family, social and national life of the people. If adaptation must tend toward the integration of worship with culture, it must seek stable cultural elements which the people can identify as their own. Liturgy must be deeply penetrated by a language and ritual which is expressive of what the people can claim as their own. Ultimately, their approval is the best proof of the validity of adaptation.

When is culture ready to pay its homage to Christ and his Church? Does adaptation require a certain phase of cultural maturity? To begin with, the notion of a developed culture is relative. As soon as cultural forms like rituals, language and art are able to express adequately a particular genius, culture is ready to be taken up into the realm of Christian worship. One must, of course, presuppose the necessary process of cleansing, or, in the words of AG 21, of healing a culture wounded by sin. One wonders if there is anything in any culture in the world that cannot be reconciled with God.

In dealing with culture one has to be aware of its religious undertones. Religion plays a decisive role in the development of culture. The Christianization of Western values and mores—and lowland Philippines typified in the city of Manila—is a remarkable example of how religion can influence culture. We witness a similar occurrence in China. Buddhism entered China around 65 A.D. By the sixteenth century it had thoroughly permeated every Chinese institution, except a sector of Chinese life and mentality which was deeply rooted in Confucianism and Taoism and which did not yield to the mystical tendency of the Indian religion.[9] We find a similar phenomenon in Europe where certain aspects of the total world-view, especially in the area of spontaneous reaction to life, have not been weaned from their pre-Christian state, although they have become integral parts of the Christian way of life.[10] But it can also happen that religion gets so engrafted to culture that culture appropriates some cultic rituals and reduces them to mere social affairs. In some traditionally Catholic countries, baptism of infants is sometimes no more than a social celebration complete with social conventions. The opposite, however, is also true. Religion sacralizes culture. It often preserves cultural forms intact and unaltered through many centuries, sometimes to the extent of reserving them for exclusive religious use. One has only to go over the pages of the history of adaptation to verify this phenomenon.

These considerations lead to the conclusion that in predominantly Christian cultures the liturgy will admit cultural forms with Christian overtones. An example of these is the Fliipino *mano po* which is a social ritual molded by Christian faith. It is a gesture of respect shown to elders and priests by touching their right hand with one's forehead. In return they give a blessing with the sign of the cross as they utter the prayer, "Kaawaan ka ng Diyos" (May God show you his kindness).[11] The adaptation of elements borrowed from cultural minority groups, as they are called in the Philippines, will smack of artificiality in solidly Christian areas. The liturgy should be in harmony with the religious culture of the people. Thus the Indian Mass adopted Hindu rituals and thought patterns. The adaptations in eucharistic celebrations for other Asian countries like Thailand will be profoundly influenced by Buddhist cultural forms.

Liturgical adaptation cannot be an isolated task. It has to be framed within the broader outlines of adaptation in the Church. The liturgy is not an independent unit of ecclesial life. The faith celebrated in the liturgy is the same faith formulated by theology. Progress in one area necessarily involves changes in the other. This is the case particularly in countries which are still neophytes in the faith. In these places the success of liturgical adaptation will depend largely on the extent of catechesis, the depth of theological reflection and the outcome of missionary efforts. Adaptation presupposes the creation of a climate favorable to it. It is told of St. Francis Xavier that, in his eagerness to adapt his language to the people, he employed Japanese words without previous catechesis. Unfortunately, the word he used to signify God had a fixed meaning in Japanese Buddhism. The saint was shocked to learn that in summoning the people to adore *Dainichi* he was actually advancing the cause of a Buddhist deity. In China, on the other hand, Matteo Ricci and his followers selected Chinese words that easily lent themselves to Christian usage. Through catechetical instruction they were able to dispel ambiguity and fill the words with Christian meaning.[12]

AG 22 offers a fresh approach to the matter when it states the necessity of stirring up theological investigation in each major socio-cultural group. This new scrutiny and rethinking should indicate the way whereby faith can be expressed according to the thought and language pattern of each major group. "As a result, avenues will be opened for a more profound adaptation in the whole area of Christian life." Liturgical adaptation has to keep pace with adaptation in theology. One does not put the cart before the horse. The lack of theological reflection can easily lead to syncretism. However, by a process of symbiosis an indigenous liturgy can contribute much to the progress of indigenous theology. Even here the axiom *lex orandi, lex credendi* is valid if the liturgy assumes native values and linguistic expressions. For if these can communicate the faith to the people in worship, they can undoubtedly serve as vehicles of the faith in theology.

All this calls for a discernment of the authenticity of cultural forms and for a process of critical evaluation. Authenticity here means that the forms correspond to and adequately express the reality experienced by the people. Critical evaluation means that they undergo the process of purification so that they can convey the Christian message. This is a task that demands not only a great respect for the traditions and genius of the people, but also an innate sensitivity to them.[13] AG 21 exhorts Christians to give expression to their faith "in the social and cultural framework of their own homeland, according to their own national traditions. They must heal and preserve it." Acquaintance is necessary for the discernment of authenticity; healing and preserving are means of critical evaluation. Perhaps only a native is able to do them. The matter is a delicate one, particularly in churches being served by foreign missionaries. In every race and culture there is always a secret chamber to which foreigners have no access. These observations, however, should not preclude the participation of foreigners in the task of adaptation. Their expertise in theology, liturgy and social sciences together with their objective assessment is as valuable a contribution as the native's role of discernment.[14]

The Three Types of Liturgical Adaptation

There are three types of liturgical adaptation. The first is *accomodatio* which touches on celebrative elements as they are performed *hic et nunc* by the liturgical assembly. This type does not necessarily involve cultural adaptation. The second type is of a cultural nature and results in a change or modification of the genius of the Roman rite. Since the Roman rite is the object of change, this type of adaptation is acculturation. The third type is also of a cultural nature and results in the reinterpretation and transformation of a pre-Christian rite in the light of Christian faith as this is celebrated by the Roman liturgy. This type of adaptation is inculturation.

In the second and third type, culture is to be understood as the sum total of a people's thought and language patterns, values and beliefs, rituals and traditions, literature and art. Underlying is the people's genius or their inner spontaneous mode of reacting to reality which finds adequate expression, according to a certain pattern, in thought which is expressed in language and translated into rituals and traditions.[15] Cultural adaptation presupposes a definition of the genius of the people and its expressions as ingredients of culture. At the same time it presupposes a knowledge of the genius of the Roman rite and its expressions in language and rituals.

The Question of Acculturation

Liturgical acculturation may be described as the process whereby cultural elements which are compatible with the Roman liturgy are incorporated into it either as substitutes or illustrations of euchological and ritual elements of the Roman rite. It is necessary that the cultural elements to be admitted should possess the connaturality to express the meaning of the Roman elements which they are to substitute or illustrate. Furthermore these cultural elements should be subjected to that process of purification whereby they acquire a Christian meaning. The process consists of re-evaluating and reinterpreting them in the light of Christian mystery and, in the manner of patristic practice, of imposing biblical typology on them.

Acculturation in the Roman liturgy shall have to take into account both the formal and the theological elements of the Roman rite. The formal elements refer to its genius of simplicity, sobriety, brevity, and practicality whether in the formulation of its euchology or in the ordering of its structure.[16] Its theological elements, on the other hand, consist of such usages in addressing the Father through the Son in the Holy Spirit.[17] Concretely, acculturation would mean inducing a change or a modification in either of these elements or in both in favor of the genius of another people. Acculturation of formal elements may be done by elaborating the Roman euchological formulas, for example, so as to suit the thought and language patterns of the people. Thus, in place of the Roman sobriety and directness, prayers may be more verbose and elaborate, appealing to sentiments more than to intellect. Historical examples of this mode of acculturation abound in the Franco-Germanic period.[18] Particular elements of culture which render this type of acculturation possible and effective are values, idiomatic expressions, maxims and proverbs. While retaining the content of Roman euchological formula, it is vehicled by such cultural ingredients.[19] Formal elements of the Roman rite may also be given a more symbolic meaning, if they merely have a practical or utilitarian character. This is the case which can be verified in the offertory procession[20] and washing of the hands at Mass.

Acculturation of theological statements, on the other hand, may be done by addressing certain prayers, excluding the eucharistic prayer, directly to Christ, as in the Gallican liturgies.[21] This would correspond to the cultural tradition of certain people with strong value of mediation. In such a tradition there is a great tendency to address Christ the Mediator directly rather than the Father. Another example is the liturgical expression of eucharistic piety, so sober and indirect in the Roman liturgy, but dramatic and elaborate in the period of the Baroque.[22]

Acculturation may use dynamic translation or dynamic equivalent.[23] Dynamic translation of a Roman text would imply the substitution of the original genius found in the text with the genius of the people. For instance, the *mirabiliter condidisti* and *mirabilius reformasti* of the Leonine Collect for Christmas,[24] which expresses the Roman reaction of awe and wonder before God's work of creation and salvation, may be translated in a dynamic fashion by using terms which express the people's spontaneous reaction to divine operations. A translation, such as "in your love you created man and in your mercy you redeemed him,"[25] stresses more the quality of a loving and merciful God than man's attitude of contemplative wonder in the face of God's work. Thus, dynamic translation goes beyond the mere employment of idiomatic expressions. It deals with the people's basic view of God, the universe and themselves.

Dynamic equivalent can be described as the assumption of rituals and traditions as substitutes or illustrations of ritual elements of the Roman rite. Concretely, it would consist of substituting Roman elements with the people's ritual ingredients that possess a similar, if not equivalent, meaning. The introductory rite of baptism, for instance, with its accent on welcome to the Church, can be given its dynamic equivalent according to the people's rituals and traditions on welcoming infants (and guests) to the family or society. The same can be said of other explanatory rites of baptism, such as the post-baptismal anointing, use of white vestment, and lighted candle. Once the theological meaning of these rites is established (priesthood, Christian dignity, living faith), the process of dynamic equivalent can begin by searching for ritual and traditional elements which express the same idea.

Dynamic equivalent can also be done through illustration. This means that the Roman rite remains intact, but acquires new cultural ingredients which serve as supplement or further illustration of the Roman ritual. This can lead to useless repetitions, especially when new rites are intended as illustra-

tions or are not sufficiently integrated into the structure of
the Roman rite. SC 65, however, seems to favor this form of
dynamic equivalent, when it says that elements from initiation rites, "when capable of being adapted to Christian ritual,
may be admitted along with those already found in Christian
tradition." If the new element is a further illustration of an
existing explanatory rite, dynamic equivalent serves only to
bridge the gap between Greco-Roman culture and the people.
On the other hand, if the new element supplements the Roman rite and gives it an additional meaning, dynamic equivalent induces the ritual and theological development of the
Roman rite.

The Question of Inculturation

Liturgical inculturation may be described as the process
whereby a pre-Christian rite is endowed with Christian meaning. The original structure of the rite together with its ritual
and celebrative elements is not subjected to radical change,
but its meaning is altered by the Church to express the Christian mystery. While acculturation induces a change or modification of the Roman genius through the assumption of new
cultural elements, inculturation brings about a change in the
culture through the entry of the Christian message. The latter
process is a form of conversion to the faith, a metanoia of pre-
Christian rites.[26]

Inculturation has several historical precedents. Baptism
and the Eucharist were pre-Christian rituals reinterpreted by
Jesus in the context of his own mystery. These were the first
instances of inculturation. The early form of Christian baptism, as described in the book of *Didaché*,[27] shows no structur-
al or ritual novelty; there was no anointing, no exorcisms,
nothing of illustrative rites of later centuries. But the meaning was radically altered. Other New Testament instances of
inculturation are the anointing of the sick, imposition of
hands, Jewish feasts and the reinterpretation of the Scriptures in the light of Christ's mystery.[28]

The present sacramental legislation, except for *Ordo Cele-*

brandi Matrimonium, does not foresee cases of inculturation. The Praenotanda of the rite of marriage, however, speaks not only of acculturation[29] but of inculturation[30] as well. This offers the possibility of drawing up a rite of marriage which suits the customs of place and people, provided that it is performed in the presence of a priest who asks for and obtains the consent of contracting parties and the nuptial blessing is imparted.[31] All this is taken from SC 77 with special reference to SC 63. Not only, therefore, may existing marriage rites in local churches be retained, as the Council of Trent legislated, but new rites which are consonant with the people's culture and traditions may be drawn up or created.[32] Furthermore, it is possible to retain traditions regarding the place of marriage and the duration of its celebration.[33] In other words, the Church, at the request of episcopal conferences and under certain canonical and liturgical conditions, can recognize marriage rites as her own sacrament. In terms of liturgical inculturation, this means that the Church enters into and penetrates a culture and, while keeping its formal expressions, radically alters its meaning. In the case of marriage the pre-Christian rite retains its cultural ingredients, but acquires a new dimension: it is the very "mystery of unity and fruitful love between Christ and the Church" signified by the sacramental pledge between husband and wife.[34]

Liturgical adaptation is a complex question.[35] It touches on theology, Christian sources, history, liturgical legislations and culture. As SC 40 has clearly foreseen, there will be greater difficulties of adaptation in mission lands, and hence there will be a need of experts who can collaborate with episcopal conferences. But the difficulty exists also in non-missionary situations where culture is evolving and there is fluidity in theological thought. This shows that adaptation is an on-going process, because both human and ecclesiastical conditions are on a process of continuous change.

Inculturation, properly done, is an ideal means of "Christianizing" the entire culture, that is to say, of imbuing culture with the spirit of Christ and his Gospel. But it is a long process which entails the gradual Christianization of diverse cultural elements through the process of acculturation. Europe can speak of Christian culture in every respect only by the thirteenth and fourteenth centuries. But by the fourteenth century the "autumn of the Middle Ages" began. Inculturation should, in other words, come about through acculturation. This will lessen the danger of religious cultural shock (as when, in hypothesis, the Church declares that the tribal marriage among Christians performed in the presence of a priest who gives the nuptial blessing is a sacrament) or of impoverishing liturgy (as in the case of the marriage rite of the Roman liturgy which simply inculturated the pre-Christian Roman marriage, thereby impoverishing the theology of Christian marriage).

Conclusion

Liturgical adaptation is a theological imperative arising from the event of the incarnation. If the Word of God became a Jew, the Church in the various countries of the world must become native to each of them. This is the principle that must underlie theological reflection, catechesis and sacramental life of the Church in every nation. The refusal to adapt amounts to a denial of the universality of salvation.

But liturgical adaptation has also its imperatives or principles. Some of them require absolute fidelity because of their relation to the basic content of divine revelation. Others have a certain fluidity and tentativeness. For the Church, like man and his culture, is never static; she is forever in the process of transition from one phase of existence to another. That is why attempts at liturgical renewal in general and adaptation in particular can never be final. One must always take them for what they are—attempts. The Counter-Reformation's *Ecclesia semper reformanda* is a principle which can be applied to the liturgy of the Church: *Liturgia semper reformanda.* In renewing the Church Vatican II renewed the liturgy first, for the Church could not acquire the vitality of the Spirit if her liturgy remained a museum piece. Today practically every liturgical rite has been revised and published in official liturgical books. This does not mean that liturgical renewal has once more come to an end and that the gains of Vatican II shall be guarded once again in the archives. As the proceedings of the meeting of the consultors of the Congregation for Divine Worship on February 21 to 22, 1978 made clear: "*Peculiaris attentio reservata est quaestioni de liturgia aptanda ad diversas culturas. Namque editis iam libris liturgicis, confectis vel fere ad finem adductis versionibus textuum liturgicorum, nonnullae Conferentiae Episcopales ad quaestiones de aptanda liturgia cura suas gradatim conferunt.*"[1] Thus, Vatican II has safeguarded the essential elements of Christian worship in view of ensuring its homogeneous growth. Continuity with the apostolic tradition is the Church's assurance that she came from Jesus Christ.

It is difficult to foretell the future of adaptation. But the Church must continue to do what she has been doing from the start: make the offer of salvation available to all men of all cultures and of all times. In performing this task she can always rely on the wisdom and power of the Holy Spirit who daily renews the face of the earth.

Notes

Chapter One

1. B. Neunheuser, *Storia della liturgia attraverso le epoche culturali,* Roma, Edizioni liturgiche, 1977, 11–14.

2. A. Nocent, *The Future of the Liturgy,* New York, Herder and Herder, 1963, 37.

3. S. Marsili, "Un Istituto Pontificio Liturgico a Roma," "Il ricorso alla storia passata, lo studio degli antichi riti, l'appello dell'archeologia fecero talvolta apparire il movimento liturgico come uno sforzo intelletuale di aspiranti archeologi, che in realtà sembravano staccarsi dalla concretezza della vita e dell'evoluzione storica. Al contrario tutto questo lavorio che rimetteva in onore le antiche fonti liturgiche, e che ad esse si ispirava per trarne principi di vita spirituale e insieme nuove visioni teologiche, si rivelò nel tempo come la scoperta di una vena di vitalità sempre valida della Chiesa," in: *Rivista Liturgica,* 48/4 (1961), 221.

4. D. S. Amalorpavadass, *Towards Indigenization in the Liturgy,* Bangalore, St. Paul Press, 1971, 174–175.

5. J. Mateos, *La célébration de la parole dans la liturgie byzantine,* Roma, Pont. Institutum Studiorum Orientalium, OCA, 191 (1971) 147; P. De Clerck, *La "prière universelle" dans les liturgies latines anciennes,* Münster, LQF, 62 (1977) 297–298.

6. R. Taft, "The Evolution of the Byzantine 'Divine Liturgy,'" in: *Orientalia Christiana Periodica,* 43 (1977) 369.

7. A. Nocent, *op. cit.,* 39–43.

8. *Ibid.,* 174–176.

9. *Ibid.,* 160.

10. *Missale Romanum ... auctoritate Pauli Pp. VI promulgatum,* Libreria Editrice Vaticana, 1975 (second edition), Institutio Generalis Missalis Romani, 52: "Deinde sacerdos manus lavat quo ritu desiderium internae purificationis exprimitur," 39.

11. S. Marsili, "Verso una teologia della Liturgia," in: *Anàmnesis,* Casale, Marietti, 1974, 1, 62–63.

12. A. Nocent, *op. cit.,* 96–100.

13. S. Safrai (ed.), *The Jewish People in the First Century,* Philadelphia, Fortress Press, 1976, II, 918–921.

14. J. H. Hertz, *The Authorized Daily Prayer Book, Hebrew Text, English Translations with Commentary and Notes.* London, Jerusalem, New York, The Soncino Press, 1976: "The language and formulae of the early Christian devotions follow Jewish models, and the forms and phrases of the synagogue liturgy reappear in the most sacred prayers of the Church": xvii.

15. W. Foerster, *From the Exile to Christ,* Philadelphia, Fortress Press, 1976 (fifth printing): "Among the many types of sacrifices, the burnt-offering took first place, while amongst the many objects of sacrifice that of atonement was paramount. Twice a day, morning and evening, a burnt-offering was made called 'the continual offering' (Heb. 'tamid'). . . . The hours of the 'Tamid-offering' were also the chief hours of prayer. In Acts III, 1 Peter and John go accordingly to the temple at the time of the afternoon 'Tamid-offering' in order to pray": 153.

16. On Stephen's address, cf. C. H. H. Scobie, "The Origins and Development of Samaritan Christianity," in: *New Testament Studies,* 19 (1972), 390–414.

17. H. Marshall, "Palestinian and Hellenistic Christianity: Some Critical Comments," in: *New Testament Studies,* 19 (1972) 271–287; A. F. J. Klijn, "The Study of Jewish Christianity," in: *New Testament Studies,* 20 (1974) 419–431; R. A. Markus, "The Problem of Self-Definition: From Sect to Church," in: E. P. Sanders (ed.), *Jewish and Christian Self-Definition,* London, SCM Press, Ltd., 1980, 1–15.

18. On the influence of the Jewish paschal meal on the Christian Eucharist, see: J. Jeremias, *The Eucharistic Words of Jesus,* London, SCM Press, Ltd., 1966, 41–88 and 218–237; of Jewish ritual baths on Christian baptism: C. Pocknee, *Water and the Spirit,* London, Darton, Longman & Todd, 1967, 17–29; of the Jewish synagogal liturgy on the Lord's Prayer: J. J. Petuchowski-M. Brocke (eds.), *The Lord's Prayer and Jewish Liturgy,* London, Burns & Oates, 1978, 3–155; of the Jewish liturgy on early Christian prayers, Amen, Trisagion, Confession and psalmody: W. E. Oesterley, *The Jewish Background of the Jewish Liturgy,* Oxford, Clarendon Press, 1925, 84–154; of Jewish feasts on Christian liturgical calendar, J. Van Goudoever, *Biblical Calendars,* Leiden, E. J. Brill, 1961, 151–260; A. Chupungco,

The Cosmic Elements of Christian Passover, Rome, Studia Anselmiana 72, Analecta Liturgica 3, 1977, 105–114; *idem,* "Feste liturgiche stagioni dell'anno," in: *Concilium,* febbraio 1981, 70–73.

19. E. Yarnold, "Baptism and the Pagan Mysteries in the Fourth Century," in: *The Heythrop Journal,* 13 (1974) 247–267.

20. S. Cavalletti, *Ebraismo e spiritualità cristiana,* Roma, Editrice Studium, 1966, 90–185.

21. M. Righetti, *Storia liturgica,* Milano, Editrice Àncora, 1949, III, 54–59.

22. D. Hill, *Greek Words and Hebrew Meanings,* Cambridge, University Press, 1967; J. M. Nielen, *Gebet und Gottesdienst im neuen Testament,* Freiburg, Herder, 1963.

23. E. Schweizer, "Il culto nel Nuovo Testamento e nell'ora attuale," in: E. Schweizer-A. Diez Macho, *La chiesa primitiva,* Brescia, Paideia Editrice, 1980, Studi Biblici 51, 55–84.

24. T. W. Guzie, *Jesus and the Eucharist,* New York, Paulist Press, 1974, 3–23.

25. C. H. Dodd, *The Founder of Christianity,* London, Collins, 1971, 91–107.

26. S. Bacchiocchi, *From Sabbath to Sunday,* Rome, The Pontifical Gregorian University Press, 1977, 132–269.

27. E. Lodi (ed.), *Enchiridion Euchologicum Fontium Liturgicorum,* Rome, Edizione Liturgiche, 1979, 19–216.

28. The synagogal *Shemôneh 'Esreh ("Eighteen Benedictions")* is now recognized as primary sources of these prayers; cf.: W. Oesterley, *op. cit.,* 122–133; L. Clerici, *Einsammlung der Zerstreuten—liturgiegeschichtliche Untersuchung zur Vor- und Nachgeschichte der Fürbitte fur die Kirche in Didache 9,4 and 10,5,* Münster, Aschendorffsche Verlagsbuchhandlung, 1966, LWQF 44, 8–102; D. C. Dulling, "The Promises to David and Their Entrance into Christianity—Nailing Down a Likely Hypothesis," in: *New Testament Studies,* 19 (1972), 55–77. Cf. also: E. Lerle, "Liturgische Reformen des Synagogengottesdienstes als Antwort auf die judenchristliche Mission des ersten Jahrhunderts," in: *Novum Testamentum,* 10 (1968) 31–42.

29. *De Baptismo,* in: R. Refoulê (ed.), *Sources Chrétiennes* 35 (1952). The Old Testament figures used by Tertullian are the water of creation (c. 3), over which the Spirit hovered (c. 4), the waters of Ex 14, 15 and 17 (c. 9), the priestly anointing of Aaron by Moses (c. 7) and the blessing of Ephraim and Manasseh (c. 8). Cf. also: P. Lundberg, *La typologie baptismale dans l'Ancienne Eglise,* Uppsala, A. B. Lundequistka Bokhandeln, 1942; J. Danielou, *The Bible and the Liturgy,*

London Darton, Longman and Todd, 1960; B. Neunheuser, *Baptism and Confirmation,* New York, Herder and Herder, 1964, 68–75.

30. Hippolytus' prayer for the ordination of bishop is inspired by biblical themes. Based on the lectures given by Professor J. Gibert in the Pontifical Liturgical Institute on the Sacrament of Holy Orders, the Old Testament references in this prayer are Psalm 112:5–6 and Daniel 13:42 in the first anamnetic portion, Exodus 29:7, Leviticus 21:10, Isaiah 61:1, Psalm 50:12–14, Jeremiah 31:31–34, and Ezechiel 36:25–28 in the second epicletic portion, and Ezechiel 34:11–19, Exodus 19:19–22, Zacharias 7:2, and Malachi 1:9 in the third intercessory portion. Cf. also P.-M. Gy, "Ancient Ordination Prayers," in: *Studia Liturgica,* 13 (1979) 86.

31. A. Chupungco, "La catechesi liturgica nella chiesa primitiva," in: *Andate e insegnate, Commento alla Catechesi Tradendae di Giovanni Paolo II,* Roma, Urbaniana University Press, 1980, 133.

32. J. Lassus, "Doura-Europos," in: F. Cabrol-H. Leclerq (eds.), *Dictionnaire d'Archeologie Chretiene et de Liturgie,* 15/2, Paris 1953, 1863–1965; A. Ferrua, "Dura Europo cristiana," in: *Civilta Cattolica,* 90/4 (1939) 334–347.

33. F. Van Der Meer-C. Mohrmann, *Bildatlas der frühchristlichen Welt,* Gutersloh, Verlaghaus G. Mohn, 1959, 33–57.

34. A.-G. Martimort, "L'Iconographie des catacombes et la catéchèse antique," in: *Rivista di Archeologia Cristiana,* 25 (1949) 105–114.

35. G. Dix, *The Shape of the Liturgy,* London, Dacre Press, 1964, 19–27.

36. A. Grabar, *L'arte paleocristiana 200–395,* Milano, Rizzoli, 1980, 59–120.

37. Ch. Delvoye, "Recherches récentes sur les origines de la basilique paleochretienne" in: *Annuaire de l'institut de philologie et d'histoire orientale et slave,* 14 (1954–1957), 205–228.

38. L. Ouspensky, *Theology of the Icon,* New York, St. Vladimir Seminary Press, 1978, "The Symbolism of the Church," 21–38.

39. "To Magnesians 6," in: P. Camelot (ed.), *Sources Chrétiennes.* 10 (1945) 70–72, also "To Trallians 2–3," 82–84; "To Smyrneans 8," 126–128.

40. C. H. Kraeling, *The Excavations at Dura-Europos, The Synagogue,* London, Oxford, New Haven, 1956; P. J-B Frey, *Corpus Inscriptionum Iudaicarum,* Roma, Pontificio Istituto di Archeologia Cristiana, 1936, I, cxviii–cxliv.

41. E. Lodi (ed.), *Enchiridion Euchologicum Fontium Liturgi-*

corum, Clavis Methodologica cum Commentariis Selectis, Bononiae, 1979, 5–22.

42. L. W. Barnard, "The Old Testament and Judaism in the Writings of Justin Martyr," in: *Vetus Testamentum* (1964) 400–401.

43. J. P. Audet, *Didaché,* Paris, J. Gabalda et Cie., 1958, 234.

44. S. Sandmel, *Judaism and Christian Beginnings,* New York, Oxford University Press, 1978, 422–423.

45. L. J. Luzbetak, *The Church and Cultures,* South Pasadena, William Carey Library, 1970: "Accommodation does not, of course, require the Church or her missionaries to 'go native' (see pp. 97, 99, 189–190). ... Accommodation calls merely for *nativization.* It requires of the Church and her missioners perfect understanding or 'empathy' (see pp. 95–97, 100–103) and, as far as possible, identification with the local cultures": 347–348.

46. J. Michell, *The Earth Spirit,* London, Thames and Hudson, 1975, 3–23: "The completely profane world, the wholly desacralized cosmos, is a recent discovery in the history of the human spirit," citing M. Eliade, *The Sacred and the Profane* (47).

47. A. Henrichs, "Pagan Ritual and the Alleged Crimes of the Early Christians," in: P. Granfield-J. A. Jungmann (eds.), *Kyriakon, Festschrift Johannes Quasten,* Münster, Verlag Aschendorff, 1970, I, 18–35.

48. J. Ching, "Confucianism: A Philosophy of Man," in: J. D. Whitehead-Y. Shaw-N. J. Girardot (eds.), *China and Christianity,* Notre Dame, Indiana, The University of Notre Dame Press, 1979, 8–34.

49. *Documentation catholique,* 909 (1939) 170.

50. A. Kavanagh, "Riti civili e riti cristiani," in: *Concilium,* febbraio 1978, 39–42.

51. T. W. Mason, "Entry into Membership of the Early Church," in: *Journal of Theological Studies,* 48 (1947) 25–33.

52. A. Quacquarelli, *Retorica e liturgia antenicena,* Roma, Desclée & Co., 1960, 303–304.

53. *Apology I, 66,* in: L. Pautigny (ed.), *Justin, Apologies,* Paris, Alphonse Picard, 1904, 140–142.

54. *De Baptismo 2,* in: R. Refoulé (ed.), *op. cit.,* 65–66.

55. *Protrepticus,* in: O. Stählin (ed.), *Die grieschen christlichen Schriftsteller der ersten drei Jahrhunderte,* Leipzig 1 (1905) 1–86.

56. Pauly-Wissowa (ed.), *Real-Encyclopedie,* 20 (1917) 1258.

57. These expressions are found respectively in *De Corona* XIII, 7: *"omnes alienae, profanae, illicitae, semel iam in sacramenti eiera-*

tae," *De Spectaculis* XXIV, 2–3: *"hoc erit pompa diaboli, adversus quam in signaculo fidei eieramus,"* *De Anima* XXXV, 3: *"Tum si in diabolum transfertur adversarii mentio ex observatione comitante, cum illo quoque moneris inire concordiam quae deputetur ex fidei conventione."*

58. *Ibid.*

59. *De Sacramentis* I, 4, in: B. Botte (ed.), *Sources Chrétiennes* 25bis (1961) 62. It is interesting to note in *De Mysteriis* VI, 30 that Ambrose follows Tertullian's biblical typology of anointing: *"Ideo in barbam defluit, id est in gratiam iuventutis, ideo in barbam Aaron ut fias electum genus, sacerdotale pretiosum."*

60. B. Botte (ed.), *La Tradition apostolique de Saint Hippolyte,* LQF 39 (1963) 56.

61. Pauly-Wissowa (ed.), *op. cit.,* 30, 1570–1571; cf. also: J. Jungmann, *The Early Liturgy,* London, Darton, Longman & Todd, 1959.

62. *Apology I,* 65, 67, in: L. Pautigny (ed.), *op. cit.,* 138, 142.

63. *Traditio Apostolica,* 9, 5, in: B. Botte (ed.), *op. cit.,* 28, 18.

64. S. S. Alexander, "Studies in Constantinian Church Architecture," in: *Rivista di Archeologia Cristiana,* 47 (1971) 281–330.

65. A. Raes, *Introductio in Liturgiam Orientalem,* Romae, Pontificium Institutum Studiorum Orientalium, 1947, 25.

66. E. Yarnold, *The Awe-Inspiring Rites of Initiation,* Slough, St. Paul Publications, 1977, 3–62.

67. *Mystagogical Catecheses,* in: A. Piédagnel (ed.), *Sources Chrétiennes* 126 (1966); *De Sacramentis,* in: B. Botte (ed.), *op cit., De Mysteriis,* in: B. Botte (ed.), *op. cit.*

68. *Ibid.*

69. Examples are (i) the anaphora of the *Apostolic Constitutions,* in: F. X. Funk (ed.), *Didascalia et Constitutiones Apostolorum,* Paderborn, F. Schoeningh, 1905, 496–515, which elaborately praises God for the work of creation, relates the history of salvation (man's creation, fall, the patriarchs, and the exodus), and after the Sanctus, recalls Christ's mystery; (ii) the anaphora of St. Mark, in: F. Brightman-C. Hammond (ed.), *Liturgies, Eastern and Western,* Oxford, Clarendon Press, 1967, I, 125–134, which also commemorates the work of creation before passing on the Christological themes; (iii) the anaphora used in fourth-century Jerusalem, which can be gathered in part from Cyril's Mystagogical Catechesis, cf.: E. J. Cutrone, "Cyril's Mystagogical Catecheses and the Evolution of the Jerusalem Anaphora," in: *Orientalia Christiana Periodica,* 44 (1978) 52–64.

70. G. Valentini—G. Caronia, *Domus ecclesiae,* Bologna, Casa

Editrice Patron, 1969, 1–52.

71. T. Matthews, "An Early Roman Chancel Arrangement and Its Liturgical Functions," in: *Rivista di Archeologia Cristiana*, 38 (1962) 81–82.

72. *Ibid.*, 83–87 on the lectern; regarding the altar, cf. O. Nussbaum, *Der Standort des Liturgen am christlichen Altar vor dem Jahre 1000*, Theophaneia 18/1, Bonn, Peter Hanstein Verlag GMBH, 1965, 269–283.

73. J. G. Davies, "Architectural Setting," in: J. G. Davies (ed.), *A Dictionary of Liturgy and Worship*, London, SCM, 1972, 21–30.

74. J. Burckhardt, *The Age of Constantine the Great*, London, Routledge and Kegan Paul, 1949, 124–214.

75. *De Sacramentis* I, 4, in: B. Botte (ed.), *op. cit.*, 62.

76. *The Second Instruction*, PG 49, 231–240; cf. also A. Hamman (ed.), *Baptism*, New York, Alba House, 1967.

77. T. Schäfer, *Die Fusswaschung*, Beuron, Beuroner Kunstverlag, 1956, 1–19.

78. The Rule of Benedict mentions also the washing of feet, probably as a sign of welcome or charity toward the monastery's guests: H. Rochais (tr.), *La Règle de Saint Benoît*, Desclée de Brouwer, 1980, 114–115.

79. *De Sacramentis* III, 5: "In omnibus cupio sequi ecclesiam Romanam, sed tamen et nos hominis sensum habemus. Ideo quod alibi rectius servatur et nos rectius custodimus," in: B. Botte (ed.), *op. cit.*, 94.

80. *De Sacramentis* III, 5, in: B. Botte (ed.), *op. cit.*, 94.

81. R. Taft, "How Liturgies Grow: The Evolution of the Byzantine 'Divine Liturgy,' " in: *Orientalia Christiana Periodica*, 48 (1977) 356.

82. G. Wilpert, *Un capitolo di storia del vestiario*, Roma, Tipografia dell'unione cooperativa Editrice, 1898, II, 61–102.

83. L. C. Mohlberg-L. Eizenhöfer-P. Siffrin (eds.), *Sacramentarium Veronense*, Rerum Ecclesiasticarum Documenta I, Roma, Herder Editrice e Libreria, 1978 (3rd edition) 118–122. These prayers were especially studied in: D. N. Power, *Ministers of Christ and His Church*, London, Geoffrey Chapman, 1969, 58–73.

84. *Ibid.*, 63 citing W. Dürig, "Dignitas," in: *Reallexikon für Antike und Christentum* III, col. 1025–35.

85. *Ibid.*, 63 citing *Thesaurus Linguae Latinae*, Leipzig, 1900, VI, 3, col. 2916 ff.

86. *Ibid.*

87. B. Botte (ed.), *La Tradition Apostolique de Saint Hippolyte*, 26–27.

88. This expression, taken from the clause "*dignisque successibus de inferiori gradu per gratiam tuam capere potiora mereantur*" of the Sacramentary of Verona's prayer for ordination to diaconate, has been replaced by "*quatenus, Filium tuum, qui non venit ministrari sed ministrare, imitantes in terris, cum ipso regnare mereantur in caelis*" in the 1968 revision of the ordination rites and prayers, wherein the ordination prayers for deacons and presbyters remain as those of the Sacramentary of Verona. The change here is explained thus: "*Mutationes maioris momenti, in hac parte prouti facile eruitur, respiciunt novam rerum condicionem promanantem ex restitutione Diaconatus permanentis: nam, hoc in casu, sermo amplius haberi nequit de capiendis potioribus de inferiori gradu, sicut habebatur in Pontificali Romano*": C. Braga, "*Adnotationes quae fontes historicos uniuscuiusque partis praebent et rationes mutationum inductarum illustrant,*" in: *Ephemerides Liturgicae*, 88 (1969) 20.

89. G. Wissowa-W. Kroll (eds.), *Paulys Real-Encyclopedie der classischen Altertumswissenschaft*, Stuttgart, J. B. Metz-Buchhandlung, 1939, XVIII–1, 930 ff.

90. J. Jungmann, *The Early Liturgy to the Time of Gregory the Great*, London, Darton, Longman & Todd, 1966, 122–123; O. Casel, *Das christliche Kultmysterium*, Regensburg, Fr. Pustet, 1960, 75–89; H. Rahner, *Greek Myths and Christian Mystery*, London, Burns & Oates, 1963.

91. J. Quasten, "Vetus Superstitio et Nova Religio: The Problem of Refrigerium in the Ancient Church of North Africa," in: *Harvard Theological Review*, 33 (1940) 253–266.

92. Ambrose's prohibition involved Augustine's mother who humbly submitted to the will of the bishop: *Confessiones* VI 2, in: P. Knöll (ed.), *Corpus Scriptorum Ecclesiasticorum Latinorum* 33 (1896) 114–116; Augustine's tolerant attitude toward *refrigerium* is shown in his *Epistularum* XXII 6, in: A. Goldbacher (ed.), *Corpus Script. Eccl. Lat.*, 34 (1895) 58–59.

93. F. Funk (ed.), *op. cit.*, II, 172–177.

94. J. Jungmann, *Missarum Sollemnia*, Wien, Verlag Herder, 1948, I, 41–42.

95. F. Cabrol, "Baiser," in: F. Cabrol (ed.), *Dictionnaire d'Archéologie Chrétienne et de Liturgie*, Paris 1910, II-1, 117.

96. J. Quasten, "A Phytagorean Idea in Jerome," in: *American Journal of Philology*, 63 (1942) 207–215.

97. Gregory of Nazianzus, *Oratio 40,* 46; *45,* 2, in: *PG,* 36, 425, 624; Gregory of Nyssa, *Oratio IV, De sancto et salutari festo Paschae,* in: *PG,* 46, 682.

98. H. M. Riley, *Christian Initiation,* in: J. Quasten (ed.), *Studies in Christian Antiquity* 17 (1974) 62–64.

99. J. Jungmann, *The Early Liturgy to the Time of Gregory the Great,* 136–137.

100. T. Klauser, *Die Cathedra in Totenkult der heidnischen und christlichen Antike,* DQF 21 (1971) 152–183.

101. T. Klauser, *A Short History of the Western Liturgy,* Oxford, Oxford University Press, 1979 (second edition) 182–183 which refer to the ff.: F. J. Dolger, *Sol salutis,* DF 4/5 (1925) 2nd ed.; investigations into the basis of the ancient practice of turning east for prayer: E. Peterson, *Frühkirche Judentum und Gnosis,* Rome-Freiburg-Vienna, 1959, 1–35.

102. B. Botte (ed.), *La Tradition Apostolique de Saint Hippolyte,* 46–47.

103. C. Vogel, "L'orientation vers l'Est du célébrant et des fideles pendant la celebration eucharistique," in: *Orient syrien,* 33 (1964) 3–38; also his article "Versus ad Orientem," in: *La Maison-Dieu,* 70 (1962), 67–99.

104. F. Dölger, *Sphragis. Eine altchristliche Taufbezeichnung in ihren Beziehungen zur profanen und religiosen Kultur des Altertums,* Paderborn 1911.

105. E. Peterson, *Pour une théologie du vêtement,* Lyons, 1943.

106. A. Croegaert, *Les rites et prières du saint sacrifice de la messe,* I, Malines 1948 (second ed.), 562–563; A. Alföldi, *Die Ausgestaltung des monarchischen Zeremoniells am römischen Kaiserhofe,* in: *Römische Mitteilungen,* 49 (1934) 111.

107. M. Andrieu, *Les Ordines Romani du haut moyen-âge,* II, *Les textes,* in: *Spicilegium sacrum lovaniense,* 23 (1948) 67–108.

108. J. Jungmann, *Missarum sollemnia,* Wien 1962 (fifth ed.) II, 3–4 where a complete presentation of offertory procession from its inception to dissolution due to rise of Mass stipend practice is given; for recent developments, see: B. Hearne, "The Significance of the 'Zaire Mass,' " in: *African Ecclesiastical Review* 17 (1975) 218.

109. C. Dereine, "La prétendue règle de Gregoire VII pour les chanoines réguliers," in: *Revue Benedictine,* 71 (1961) 108–118.

110. C. Vogel, *Introduction aux sources de l'histoire du culte chrétien au moyen âge,* Spoleto, Centro Italiano di Studi sull' Medioevo, 1975, 206.

111. M. Midali, "La tradizione liturgica alla quarta sessione del Concilio di Trento (7 febbraio-8 aprile 1546)" in: *Ephemerides Liturgicae*, 87 (1973) 501–525.

112. E. Cattaneo, *Il culto cristiano in occidente*, Roma, Edizioni liturgiche, 1978, 523–524.

113. G. Every, *The Mass*, Dublin, Gill and Macmillan, 1978, 156–194.

114. A. Baumstark, *Vom geschichtlichen Werden der Liturgie*, Ecclesia Orans 10, Freiburg i. Br., 1923, 37–47.

115. N. M. Denis-Boulet-R. Beraudy, *The Eucharist*, in: A. G. Martimort, *The Church at Prayer*, Shannon, Irish University Press, 1973, 26.

116. K. Gamber, *Codices Liturgici Latini Antiquiores*, Spicilegii Friburgensis Subsidia 1, Freiburg Schweiz 1968, I, 132, 140, 156–170, 196–207, 230–237, 262–270, 294–318; Vol. II, 325–428.

117. *Ibid.*, Vol. I, 174–180, 214–219, 270–275; Vol. II, 429–491.

118. *Ibid.*, Vol. I, 145–150, 220–223, 250–254, 275–278; Vol. II, 492–526.

119. M. Andrieu, *Les Ordines Romani du haut moyen-âge*, I, *Les manuscrits*, Spicilegium Sacrum Lovaniense, II (1930); II, *Les textes* (*Ordines I-XIII*), 23 (1948); III, *Les textes* (*Ordines XIV–XXXIV*), 24 (1958), IV, *Les textes* (*Ordines XXXV–XLIX*), 28 (1956); V, *Les textes* (*Ordo L*), 29 (1961).

120. O. Casel, *Das christliche Opfermysterium. Zur Morphologie und Theologie des eucharistichen Hochgebetes*, Graz 1968, 215–380.

121. T. Federici, "Le liturgie dell'area orientale," in: *Anàmnesis*, Casale, Marietti editori, 1978, vol. 2, 113–116.

122. O. H. E. Khs-Burmester, *The Egyptian or Coptic Church*, Cairo, Printing Office of the French Institute of Oriental Archeology, 1967, 48.

123. G. A. Maloney, "Ethiopian Rite," in: *New Catholic Encyclopedia*, New York, McGraw-Hill Book Company, 1967, vol. 5, 587.

124. C. Mohrmann, "Epiphania," in: *Ètudes sur le Latin des chrétiens*, Roma, Edizioni di Storia e Letteratura, 1961 (Deuxième Edition), vol I, 263–264.

125. B. Capelle, "Le Kyrie de la messe et le pape Gélase," in: *Revue Bénédictine*, 46 (1934) 126–144.

126. B. Capelle, "Le texte du Gloria in excelsis Deo," in: *Revue d'histoire ecclesiastique*, 44 (1949) 439–457.

127. *Epist. 64*, Lib. XI, *PL* 77, col. 1187; cf. also: D. Norberg, *In Registrum Gregorii Magni Studia Critica*, I (Uppsala 1937) 133.

128. P. Meyvaert, "Diversity within Unity, A Gregorian Theme," in: *The Heythrop Journal*, 4 (1963).

129. *Ibid.*, for Latin and English texts, 144.

130. F. Cabrol, "Les origines de la liturgie gallicane," in: *Revue d'histoire ecclesiastique*, 26 (1930) 960–961.

131. J. Quasten, "Oriental Influence in the Gallican Liturgy," in: *Traditio*, I (1943), on *trisagion*, see pp. 57–66; on litanies, see pp. 66–69; on offertory entrance, see pp. 70–71.

132. A. King, *Liturgies of the Past*, London, Longmann, Green and Co., 1959, 77–183.

133. For an example of this trend, see: A. Nocent, *The Liturgical Year*, Collegeville, The Liturgical Press, 1977, vol. 2, where the development of the Rite of Holy Thursday Reconciliation of Penitents is given, 203–214.

134. J. Deshusses (ed.), *Le Sacramentaire Grégorien*, Spicilegium Friburgense 16 (1971) 189.

135. L. C. Mohlberg (ed.), *Missale Gallicanum Vetus*, Rerum Ecclesiasticarum Documenta III (1958) 42.

136. For a description of the classical form of the Roman liturgy according to the original Roman genius, see: E. Bishop, "The Genius of the Roman Rite," in his book: *Liturgica Historica*, Oxford, Clarendon Press, 1918, 1–19.

137. After a visit to Rome in 781 Emperor Charlemagne requested Pope Hadrian I for a copy of a sacramentary currently in use in Rome, in order to solve the problem of liturgical confusion brought about by the Gelasian Sacramentaries of the eighth century. The letter of Pope Hadrian I is preserved; see: *Ep. III*, in: *Monumenta Germanica Historica*, Hanover 1826.

138. J. Deshusses (ed.), *Le Sacramentaire Grégorien, "Hadrianum Revisum Anianense cum supplemento,"* 351–605.

139. Although one can speak of the Franco-Germanization of the Roman rite, it is equally possible to speak of the Romanization of Gallican liturgies as it was expressed by C. Vogel, "Les motifs de la romanisation du culte sous Pépin le bref et Charlemagne," in: *Culto cristiana, Politica imperiale carolingia*, Todi, L'Accademia Tudertina, 1979, 15–41.

140. A. Nocent, "Storia dei libri liturgici romani," in: *Anàmnesis* 2, 166–167.

141. C. Vogel-R. Elze (eds.), *Le Pontifical romano-germanique du dixième siècle*, Studi e testi 227 (1963), vols. I–II.

142. G. M. Dreves, (ed.), *Hymnarius Moisiacensis. Das Hymnar*

der Abtei Moissac im 10. Jahrhundert, in: *Analecta Hymnica Medii Aevi* 2 (Leipzig 1888) where we find data about *Veni Creator,* pp. 93–94, and *Ut queant laxis,* ascribed to a *poetae latini aevi Carol.,* pp. 50–51; Cl. Blume-H. M. Bannister (eds.), *Liturgische Prosen des Übergangsstiles und der zweiten Epoche insbesondere die dem Adam von Sankt Victor,* in: *Analecta Hymnica* 54/1 (Leipzig 1915) where we find data about *Victimae paschali laudes, nach 1048,* pp. 12–14.

143. S. Bottari (ed.), *Tesori d'arte cristiana, il romanico,* Bologna, Officine grafiche Poligrafici il Resto del Carlino, 1966, vol. 2, pp. 85–112, 141–196, 477–504, 533–560.

144. O. Nussbaum, *Kloster, Priestermönch und Privatmesse,* in: *Theophaneia* 14 (Bonn, 1961), 96–177.

145. J. Eminghaus, *The Eucharist,* Collegeville, The Liturgical Press, 1978, 78.

146. Cf., the unpublished work of J. Döring, *Die Privatmesse. Ein Versuch zur soziologie der frühchristlichen Liturgik* (Marburg, 1925) cited by O. Nussbaum, *op. cit.,* 170–171.

147. R. Bainton, *The Church of Our Fathers,* New York, Charles Scribner's Sons, 1969 (republication of 1941 work) where the period is described as time of "mighty deeds": 93.

148. E. Cattaneo, *op. cit.,* 234.

149. Gregory VII, *Regula Canonica*; cf. G. Morin,"Etudes, textes, découvertes," in: *Anecdota Maredsolana* (Paris 1913) 459–460; the twelfth-century Roman Pontifical can be found in M. Andrieu (ed.), *Le Pontifical romain au moyen-âge,* Studi e testi 86 (1938), tome I.

150. V. Kennedy, "The Moment of Consecration and the Elevation of the Host," in: *Mediaeval Studies* 6 (Toronto 1944) 121–150.

151. M. Righetti, *Storia liturgica, III—L'Eucaristia,* Milano, Editrice Ancora, 1948, 328–330.

152. S. Bottari (ed.), *op. cit., il gotico,* vol. 3, pp. 29–58, 85–112, 141–168, 253–280, 337–364.

153. M. Andrieu, *op. cit.,* Studi e testi 87 (1940) tome II, *Le Pontifical de la Curie Romaine au XIIIe siècle,* 311–312.

154. S. J. P. Van Dijk-J. H. Walker, *The Origins of the Modern Roman Liturgy,* London, Darton, Longman & Todd, 1960: ". . . the Roman liturgy . . . in the hands of the Friar Minors became the official worship of the Roman Christendom. Indeed, the Western Schism, the sword between the Middle Ages and the Renaissance, prevented it from becoming the liturgy of the people. This again is another story in which the official prayer of the clergy became a closed book to the laity. But if Christendom and public worship are again social prob-

lems in the West, the lesson of the thirteenth century is as topical now as it was then": 417–418.

155. J. Huizinga, *The Waning of the Middle Ages,* London, Edward Arnold, 1976 (reprint of 1924 edition) 182–205.

156. C. Lange, *Die lateinischen Osterfeiern,* München, Verlag von Ernst Stahl sen., 1887, 79 ff.

157. W. Lipphardt, "Der dramatische Tropus. Fragen des Ursprungs der Ausführung und der Verbreitung," in: AA. VV., *Dimensioni drammatiche della liturgia medievale,* Acts of the First Gathering for Study held at Viterbo on May 31 until June 2, 1976, Viterbo, Bulzoni Editore, 1977, 17–31.

158. An example of an apocryphal story that provided an item for dramatization is the burial of the Blessed Virgin on the day of her Dormition; cf., C. Tischendorf (ed.), *Apocalypses Apocryphae,* Leipzig. 1866; "Dormitio Mariae," 95ff.; the dramatization can be found in "Ordinarius canonicorum ecclesiae Assindensis de officiatione monasterii"; cf. F. Arens (ed.), *Der Liber der Essener Stiftskirche,* Paderborn, Druck und Verlag, 1908, 104–106.

159. *Ibid.*; the dramatization of the ascension by bringing up the cross toward a designated altar shrine was done before the High Mass: 88–89.

160. R. B. Donavan, *The Liturgical Drama in Medieval Spain,* Toronto, Pontifical Institute of Mediaeval Studies, 1958, 6–19.

161. This meeting is mentioned in E. Horn, *Iconographiae Monumentorum Terrae Sanctae (1724–1744),* edited by E. Foade, Jerusalem, Franciscan Press, 1962: "*De loco apparitionis Magdalenae et de sacello B.V. de apparitione: . . . per annum manet clausum obducta pictura repraesentante apparitionem Christi post resurrectionem suam B.M. Virgini factam: per quam datur intelligere quod ideo erectum sit illud altare, quia pie creditur in eo loco Christum Dominum post gloriosam resurrectionem dilectissimae Matri suae prima apparuisse: quod communis in his partibus traditio Catholicorum tenet*": 100–101; this tradition is part of the epic poetry in several Philippine languages that possess the narration of the creation and fall, the coming of Christ and his redemptive work, and the finding of the cross and the second coming—all in verses sung during Lenten season by the Catholic folks from the book (whose author is unknown) entitled *Pasiong Mahal ni Hesukristong Panginoon natin,* Manila, 1977 (reprint of the 1884 edition) 181–182; cf. also M. Andrade, "Encuentro during Easter Sunday Celebration," in: *The Liturgical Information Bulletin of the Philippines,* VI (March–April 1971) 32–33.

162. E. O. James, *Seasonal Feasts and Festivals,* New York, Barnes & Noble, Inc., 1963, 26.

163. As an interpretative help, the dramatic reading of the Gospel and other biblical pericopes that might lend themselves to such approach is suggested as feasible enhancement for the comprehension of children: "... *magni aestimanda sunt omnia elementa, quae interpretationi lectionum inserviunt ... Ubi textus id suadet, utile potest ut ipsi pueri (lectores) eum distributis partibus legant, quemadmodum pro lectione Passionis Domini in Hebdomada Sancta statutum est"*, Directorium de Missis cum pueris, 47, in: *Acta Apostolicae Sedis,* 66 (1974) 43.

164. Mpongo Mpoto Mamba, "Evangélisation et liturgie," in: *Telema,* 2 (1976): *"De ces considerations il resulte que l'expression humaine ne se réduit pas à l'oralité et, encore moins, au langage conceptuel. Elle comprend également des representations et suppose le recours au langage symbolique";* 14.

165. J. Jungmann, "The State of Liturgical Life on the Eve of the Reformation," in: *Pastoral Liturgy,* London, Challoner, 1962, 64–80.

166. *Ibid.*

167. B. Neunheuser, *L'eucharistie,* Paris, Les éditions du Cerf, 1966, 95–102.

168. It legislated, however, the possibility that new rites consonant with the people's culture and traditions may be drawn up (*Concilii Tridentini Decretum de Reformatione Matrimonii "Tametsi"* I, in: Mansi 33, 153) but as SC 77 quotes it, the implementation has still to be seen.

169. Mansi, 33, 194.

170. T. Klauser, "Rigid Unification in the Liturgy and Rubricism," in: *A Short History of the Western Liturgy,* 129–155; there were instances, however, of allowance for local rituals but regarding the celebration of the Eucharist the observations on rubricism are evident.

171. B. Häring, *The Sacraments in a Secular Age,* Slough, St. Paul Publications, 1976, 2–5.

172. J. Kramp, "Die eucharistiche Huldigung in Gegenwart und Geschichte," in: *Stimmen der Zeit,* 53 (1923) 161–176.

173. J. Jungmann, *The Mass of the Roman Rite,* New York, 1961 (one volume abridged edition), 112; see also: *idem,* "Liturgical Life in the Baroque Period," in: *Pastoral Liturgy,* 80–101; A. Mayer, *Die Liturgie in der europäischen Geistesgeschichte,* Darmstadt 1971, 97–154.

174. Both the Catholics and Protestants breathed the air of the Baroque period; cf.: E. Routley, *Church Music and Christian Faith,* London, Collins, 1980 (second edition), 21–29, 50–63.

175. P. Salmon, *The Breviary through the Centuries,* Collegeville, Liturgical Press, 1962, 88–93.

176. C. Bolton, *Church Reform in the 18th-Century Italy (The Synod of Pistoia, 1786),* The Hague, Nijhoff, 1969, 55–114.

177. A. Meyer, *op. cit.,* 311.

178. L. Soltner, *Solesmes & Dom Gueranger,* 1805–1875, Solesmes, M. Lescuyer et Fils, 1974, 7.

179. R. W. Franklin, "Guéranger and Pastoral Liturgy: A Nineteenth Century Context," in: *Worship,* 50 (1976) 157.

180. *Idem,* "Guéranger: A View on the Centenary of His Death," *ibid.,* 49 (1975) 318–328.

181. *La restaurazione liturgica nell'opera di Pio XII. Atti del primo congresso internazionale di liturgia pastorale.* Assisi-Roma, 18–22 settembre 1956, Genova 1957, concluding section.

182. L. Beauduin, *Vida Litúrgica,* Coleçao "Liturgica" IV (1938) 17–23, 113–123; A. Haquin, *Dom Lambert Beauduin et le Renouveau Liturgique,* Recherches et synthèses, Histoire 1, Gembloux, Duculot, 1970, 226–228.

183. *Acta Apostolicae Sedis,* 56 (1964) 97–134.

184. F. Bontinck, *La lutte autour de la liturgie chinoise aux XVIIe et XVIIIe siècles,* Louvain, Editions Nauwelaerts, 1962; G. Dunne, *Generation of Giants,* Indiana, University of Notre Dame Press, 1962; F. Bortone, *P. Matteo Ricci S. I. Il "Saggio d'Occidente,"* Roma, Desclée & C., 1965; A. Rowbotham, *Missionary and Mandarin,* New York, Russel and Russel, 1966; J. Dournes, *L'Offrande des peuples,* Paris, Les Editions du Cerf, 1967.

185. F. Bortone, *I Gesuiti alla corte di Pechino 1601–1813,* Roma, Desclée & Co., 1969, 141–184.

186. *Doctrina Christiana: The First Book Printed in the Philippines, Manila 1593,* Manila, National Historical Commission, 1973.

187. V. Cronin, *The Wise Man from the West,* London, Rupert Hart-Davis, 1959, 200–202.

188. J. Ching, "Confucianism: A Philosophy of Man," in: J. Whitehead, Y.-M. Shaw, N. Girardot (eds.), *China and Christianity,* Indiana, University of Notre Dame Press, 1979, 21.

189. F. Bortone, *I Gesuiti alla corte di Pechino 1601–1813,* 145.

190. *Ibid.*

191. *Ibid.,* 181, citing A. S. Rosso, *Apostolic Legations to China of*

the Eighteenth Century, South Pasadena, 1948; an original version of the graph is to be found in *Bibliotheque National de Paris*.

192. "Instructio Vicariorum Apostolicorum ad Regna Synarum Tonchini et Cocinnae Proficiscentium," in: *Collectanea Sacrae Congregationis de Propaganda Fide*, I, Rome, 1907.

193. *Acta Apostolicae Sedis*, 31 (1939) 429.

194. *Ibid.*, 32 (1940) 24–26.

195. *Documentation catholique*, 99 (1939) 170.

196. The importation of basilica style of building churches in Ethiopia took place in the earliest period of evangelization in Axum and only later did the acceptance of native architecture take place, cf.: S. Denyer, *African Traditional Architecture*, London, Heinemann, 1978, 53–54, 98.

197. J. Dourne, *op. cit.*, 133.

198. J. Knox, "Relatio de laboribus et inceptis Sacrae Congregationis pro Cultu divino et Synodus Episcoporum 1974," in: *Notitiae*, 10 (1974) 355–356.

199. *Ibid.*, 358–359.

Chapter Two

1. Paulus VI, "Constitutio Apostolica, Missale Romanum": "Per quattuor enim saecula, non modo illud ritus latini sacerdotes pro norma habuerunt, ad quam eucharisticum sacrificium facerent, sed sacri etiam Evangelii nuntii in omnes fere terras invexerunt": in *Ordo Missae, Missale Romanum*, Typis Polyglottis Vaticanis 1975, 11.

2. *Ibid.*: "Haud secus Nos, etsi, de praescripto Concilii Vaticani II, in novum Missale *legitimas varietates et aptationes* (SC 38–40) ascivimus, nihilo tamen secius fore confidimus, ut hoc ipsum a christifidelibus quasi subsidium et ad mutuam omnium unitatem testandam confirmandamque accipiatur": 12.

3. E. Bishop, *Liturgica Historica*, Oxford, Clarendon Press, 1918, 12.

4. A. Chupungco, "The Magna Carta of Liturgical Adaptation," in: *Notitiae* 139 (1978) 75.

5. *Acta Apostolicae Sedis*, 31 (1939) 429.

6. R. Kaczynski (ed.), *Enchiridion Documentorum Instaurationis Liturgicae*, Rome, Marietti, 1976, 10.

7. *Schema Constitutionis de Sacra Liturgia*, Typis Polyglottis Vaticanis 1962, "Emend. IV," 15.

8. *Ibid.*

9. *Ibid.,* "Modi I, Prooemium-Caput I": "Periculosum videtur permittere mutationes in ipsa liturgia derivatas ex moribus populorum, nam ansa dabitur destructioni ritus latini": 25.

10. *Ibid.,* "Emend. IV, Appendix": The Conciliar Commission explained that on matters of faith a *rigidior aut etiam absoluta unitas* is required; on matters not touching the faith but the common good *aliqua plus minusve extensa aut rigida unitas* is necessary: 27.

11. *Ibid.,* 16.

12. *Ordo Baptismi Parvulorum,* Typis Polyglottis Vaticanis 1973 (second edition), nn. 30–35, pp. 12–13.

13. B. Luykx, "The Impact of the Liturgical Documents," in: *African Ecclesiastical Review,* 13 (1971) 97–107.

14. *Schema,* "Emend. IV, Appendix," 27.

15. *Ibid.,* 16. The proposed text read: "Et quia in quibusdam regionibus, praesertim autem in Missionibus, Liturgiae aptatio difficilior evadit et magis urget. . . ." The revised text reads: "Cum tamen variis in locis et adiunctis, profundior liturgiae aptatio urgeat, et ideo difficilior evadat. . . ."

16. A. King, *Liturgies of the Past,* London, Longmans, Green and Co., Ltd., 1959, *passim.*

17. C. Vogel, "Les motifs de la romanisation du culte sous Pépin le Brief (751) et Charlemagne (774–814)," in *AA. VV. Culto Cristiano Politica Imperiale Carolingia,* L'Academia Tudertina, 1979, 15–41.

18. L. Soltner, *Solesmes & Dom Guéranger, 1805–1875,* Solesmes 1974, 67.

19. C. Vagaggini, *Il Senso teologico della liturgia,* Rome, Edizioni Paoline, 1965, 310–312.

20. Cf. SC 44: "It is desirable that the competent territorial ecclesiastical authority mentioned in Article 22, 2, set up a liturgical commission, to be assisted by experts in liturgical science, sacred music, art, and pastoral practice."

21. A. Chupungco (ed.), *Liturgical Renewal in the Philippines, Maryhill Liturgical Consultations,* Quezon City 1980, 3, 111, 181.

22. X. Seumois, "Norme per adattare la liturgia al carattere ed alle tradizioni dei diversi popoli," in: V. Joannes (ed.), *Commento alla Costituzione sulla Liturgia,* Brescia, Editrice Queriniana, 1965, 109; A. Botero, "Principios para la adaptacion liturgica en las culturas nativas," in: *Notitiae* 99 (1974) 384–390. Botero follows closely the severity of Seumois, which seems to be the attitude of the Congregation for Divine Worship at that time. For a more liberal stand see:

C. Braga, "Un problema fondamentale di pastorale liturgica: adatta-mento e incarnazione nelle varie culture," in: *Ephemerides Liturgi-cae* 89 (1975) 5–39.

23. J. G. Frazer, *The Golden Bough,* London, Macmillan & Co., Ltd., 1963 (abridged edition): "The same idea comes out in the Ger-man and French custom of the Harvest-May. This is a large branch or a whole tree, which is decked with ears of corn, brought home on the last waggon from the harvest-field, and fastened on the roof of the farmhouse or of the barn" (156). "In some villages of the Vosges Mountains on the first Sunday of May young girls go in bands from house to house, singing a song in praise of May, in which mention is made of the 'bread and meal that come in May.' . . . In the French de-partment of Mayenne, boys who bore the name of *Maillotins* used to go about from farm to farm on the first of May singing carols, for which they received money or a drink; they planted a small tree or a branch of a tree" (160). "At Bordeaux on the first of May the boys of each street used to erect in it a May-pole, which they adorned with garlands and a great crown; and every evening during the whole of the month the young people of both sexes danced singing about the pole" (163). "The wreath is dedicated in church . . . and on Easter Eve the grain is rubbed out of it by a seven-year-old girl and scattered amongst the young corn. At Christmas the straw of the wreath is placed in the manger to make the cattle thrive" (527). Cf. E. O. James, *Seasonal Feasts and Festivals,* New York, Barnes & Noble, Inc., 1963 (third edition), 291–319.

24. J. Dournes, *L'offrande des peuples,* Paris, Éditions du Cerf, 1967, "Querelle pour des rites," 127–137.

25. G. W. Buchanan, "Worship, Feasts and Ceremonies in the Early Jewish-Christian Church," in: *New Testament Studies,* 26 (1980): "The fall of Jerusalem taught them (Jewish-Christians) to ad-just their worship practices according to Jewish traditions which deemed the temple unnecessary, but they continued to mourn for it and hope for its restoration": 297.

26. A. Chupungco, "Filippine: cultura e liturgia cristiana," in: *Concilium,* febbraio 1977, "Infatti l'usanza di aspergere le fonda-menta della casa con il sangue di un pollo è un residuo dell'animismo che ancora sopravvive in una città come Manila": 104 (274).

27. *Documentation Catholique,* 93 (1939) 170.

28. G. W. Buchanan, *The Consequences of the Covenant,* Leiden, E. J. Brill, 1970, 218–219, where the argument presented points to the consideration that the Israelites' entry into the covenant by three

commandments parallels the case of the proselytes initiated via circumcision, baptism and a gift, and while this had been for some time the standard practice among the Jews and Jewish-Christians, Paul eventually convinced some churches of Asia Minor that circumcision was not needed as *initiatory* rite. Cf. N. J. McEleney, "Conversion, Circumcision and the Law," in: *New Testament Studies* 20 (1974), where among many enlightening items two particularly related matters emerge: (i) the reason for circumcision included the redemptive aspect linked with the shedding of blood (Ex. 4:24–26; 24:8) (344) and Christ's death on the cross is the Gentile's circumcision (339); (ii) Saint Paul's presentation of the teaching that God justifies the uncircumcised Gentiles through faith (Rom. 3:30) did not overthrow the law (Rom. 3:31) but rather upheld it, for circumcision "*was and is* of great value" (Rom. 2:25—3:1–2), but now salvation through faith was offered also to the Gentiles without circumcision because they are like Abraham in believing God's promises even before being circumcised (Rom. 4:1–12) (336).

29. R. J. Daly, *The Origins of the Christian Doctrine of Sacrifice,* London, Darton, Longman & Todd Ltd., 1978, 69.

30. F. Conybeare (ed.), *Rituale Armenorum,* Oxford, Clarendon Press, 1905, 55–57.

31. J. Gelineau, "The Symbols of Christian Initiation," in: W. Reedy (ed.), *Becoming A Catholic Christian,* New York, Sadlier, 1979: "What comes first is the rite. . . . This is what is primary. . . . Through the existence of a rite the subject comes to discover or perceive a meaning for an experience" (192). "Words cannot take the place of non-verbal experience in the liturgy" (193).

32. "De Initiatione Christiana, Praenotanda Generalia," IV—De aptationibus quae conferentiis episcopalibus competunt, 30, 2, in: *Ordo Baptismi Parvulorum,* 12.

33. *Ibid.,* IV, 31, p. 13.

Chapter Three

1. A. Chupungco, *Towards a Filipino Liturgy,* Manila, 1976, 45.

2. C. Vagaggini, *Il senso teologico della liturgia,* 290–297; Y. Raguin, "Indigenization of the Church" in: *Teaching All Nations,* 6 (1969) 151–168; I. Omaecheverria, "The Dogma of the Incarnation and the Adaptation of the Church to Various Peoples," in: *Omnis Terra,* 73 (1976) 277–283.

3. Pastoral Constitution on the Church in the Modern World, GS 58, "For God, revealing himself to his people to the extent of a full

manifestation of himself in his Incarnate Son, has spoken according to the culture proper to different ages."

4. D. Amalorpavadass, *Towards Indigenization in the Liturgy*, Bangalore, St. Paul Press, 1971, 14–20; O. Dominguez, "Ecclesial Indigenization: Vital Prerequisite for Catholicism," in: *Omnis Terra*, 73 (1976) 285–289.

5. S. Brechter, "Decree on the Church's Missionary Activity," in: Vorgrimler (ed.), *Commentary on the Documents of Vatican II*, New York, Herder and Herder, 1967, 87–181.

6. Reference is made to LG 13 where this citation is given: cf. St. Irenaeus, *Adv. haer.* III, 16, 6; III, 22, 1–3: PG 7, 925 C-926 A and 955 C-958.

7. J. Daniélou, "Vatican II et les nouvelles Eglises," in: *Revue du Clergé Africain*, 24 (1969) 203–212.

8. Paul VI, "Letter to the Asian Bishops," in: *L'Osservatore Romano*, April 21, 1974.

9. "Instructio Vicariorum Apostolicorum ad Regna Synarum Tonchini et Cocinnae Proficiscentium," in: *Collectanea Sacrae Congregationis de Propaganda Fide*, I, Rome 1907.

10. *I Apology 67*, 142.

11. J. Jungmann, *The Mass of the Roman Rite:* "It is plain that wherever the Old Testament appears in the readings of the fore Mass, it is not for its own sake, nor simply to have some spiritual text for reading, but it is chosen for its prophetic worth and its value as an illustration of the New Testament": 273–274.

12. D. Amalorpavadass, *Towards Indigenization in the Liturgy*, 51–52.

13. C. Vogel, *Introduction aux sources de l'histoire du culte chrétien au moyen âge*, Spoleto 1975: "Pour l'histoire du culte chrétien notre periode est capitale: la liturgue latine qui s'est fixée à cette époque (*Hadrianum* supplémenté par Alcuin vers 801–804; Pontifical romano-germanique vers 950), et qui continue d'être celle de Eglise latine d'Occident, n'est pas purement romaine; elle est mixte, hybride ou, si l'on préfère, romano-franque, voire romano-germanique": 43–44.

14. "Pour une liturgie pleinement rénovée, on ne pourra pas se contenter de textes traduits à partir d'autres langues. De nouvelles creations seront nécessaires. Il reste que la traduction des textes émanant de la tradition de l'Eglise constitue une excellente discipline et une nécessaire école à la rédaction de textes nouveaux": *Instruc-*

tions officielles sur les nouveaux rites de la messe, le calendier, les traductions liturgiques, Paris 1969, 205.

15. GS 58: "Living in various circumstances during the course of time, the Church, too, has used in her preaching the discoveries of different cultures to spread and explain the message of Christ to all nations, to probe it and more deeply understand it, and to give it better expression in the liturgical celebrations and in the life of the diversified community of the faithful."

Chapter Four

1. A. Baumstark, *Liturgie comparée,* Chevetogne 1939, "Les lois de l'evolution liturgique," 16–32.

2. A. Verheul, *Introduction to the Liturgy,* London, Burns & Oates, 1968: ". . . the meeting between God and his Church is the prime criterion of what is liturgical": 33.

3. Cf. Praefatio I de Passione Domini: "Quia per Filii tui salutiferam passionem totus mundus sensum confitendae tuae maiestatis accepit, dum ineffabili crucis potentia iudicium mundi et potestas emicat Crucifixi"; Praefatio Paschalis V: "Qui, oblatione corporis sui, antiqua sacrificia in crucis veritate perfecit, et, seipsum tibi pro nostra salute commendans, idem sacerdos, altare et agnus exhibuit": *Missale Romanum . . . auctoritate Pauli PP, VI promulgatum,* Libreria Editrice Vaticana, 1975 (second edition), 403, 409.

4. SC 7.

5. G. Fourez, "Prayer and Celebration in the Christian Community," *Worship,* 46 (1972) 141–149; P. Regan, "Liturgy and the Experience of Celebration," *Worship,* 47 (1973) 592–600; C. Rivers, *Celebration,* New York, Herder and Herder, 1969, 29–39.

6. J. Mateos, *Cristianos en fiesta,* Madrid, Ediciones Cristiandad, 1972: "Las comunicaciones intensivas de nuestra época no producen unión" (249). "La falta de meditación e intuición priva al hombre de sus experiencias profundas, las que tiene que expresar en la fiesta" (256), "La actitud escéptica, la del hombre sin ninguna fe, es sofocante" (256).

7. I. Dalmais, "The Liturgy and the Deposit of Faith," in A. G. Martimort (ed.), *The Church at Prayer,* Dublin, Irish University Press, 1968, 212–219; cf. *Concilium,* February 1973; G. Lukken, "The Unique Expression of Faith in the Liturgy," (11–21), B. Vawter-E. Villanova, "The Development of the Expression of Faith in the Worshipping Community" (23–39), J. P. Manigne-J. Ladriere-L. Gilkey,

"Language of Worship" (40–76), D. Power, "Two Expressions of Faith: Worship and Theology" (95–103).

8. SC 33.

9. Ioannes Paulus II, *Catechesi Tradendae,* Typis Polyglottis Vaticanis, 1979, art. 23, p. 23. Cf. A. Chupungco, "Elementi di Catechesi Sacramentale," in: *Andate e Insegnate, Commento alla Catechesi Tradendae di Giovanni Paolo II,* Rome, Urbaniana University Press, 1980, 287–300.

10. *Ibid.,* A. Chupungco, "La catechesi liturgica nella Chiesa primitiva," catechesi mistagogica, 138–139.

11. *Ibid.,* catechesi preparatoria, 133–138.

12. B. De Clercq, "Political Commitment and Liturgical Celebration," in: *Concilium,* April 1973, 110–116. Cf., *Concilium,* February 1974, H. Schmidt, "Lines of Political Action in Contemporary Liturgy" (13–33), J. Llopis, "The Message of Liberation in the Liturgy" (65–73), J. Gelineau, "Celebrating the Paschal Liberation" (107–119). Also A. Vannuchi, "Liturgy and Liberation," in: *International Review for Mission,* 65 (1976) 189–195.

13. S. Marsili, "La teologia della liturgia nel Vaticano II," in: *Anàmnesis,* Turin, Marietti, 1974, I, 96–100. Cf. O. Müller, "The Paschal Mystery and Its Celebration during the Liturgical Year and in the Sunday Masses," in: W. Barauna, (ed.), *The Liturgy of Vatican II,* Chicago, Franciscan Herald Press, 1966, 210–230.

14. J. D. Crichton, "A Theology of Worship," in: C. Jones *et al.* (eds.), *The Study of the Liturgy,* London, SPCK, 1978, 5–29.

15. O. Casel, *Das christliche Kultmysterium,* Regensburg, Verlag F. Pustet, 1960, 25–74.

16. A. Nocent, *The Liturgical Year,* Collegeville, The Liturgical Press, 1977, vol. I: "From the Vigil on, then, Christmas evidently celebrates a threefold mystery: the coming of Christ on earth, the mystery of his death and resurrection (the redemptive act for which he comes), and his return for judgment. The opening prayer of the Christmas Vigil Mass pulls this theology together: 'God, our Father, every year we rejoice as we look forward to this feast of our salvation. May we welcome Christ as our Redeemer, and met him with confidence when he comes to be our judge' ": 197.

17. *Ibid.,* vol. II: "The liturgy of the word on Good Friday is marked by a notable restraint. The severity, which also shows in the outward decor (the altar is completely bare, without cross, candlesticks, or cloths), could be misleading; it might induce a dramatic sense of sadness and make us forget that the death of Christ is in fact

a triumph. . . . In any case, the prayer that follows the moment of recollection at the beginning of the service expresses in a balanced way the meaning of all that is to follow . . . the mystery of the victorious Passover that is the source of our new life. The whole history of salvation is thus summed up in a few words at the moment when the Church is ready to celebrate the death of her Christ, something she cannot do without at the same time celebrating his triumph and ours": 82–83.

18. Praefatio Paschalis I; "Ipse enim verus est Agnus qui abstulit peccata mundi. Qui mortem nostram moriendo destruxit, et vitam resurgendo reparavit," *Missale Romanum,* 405.

19. A. Chupungco, "Een experiment: De Filippijnse mis," in: A. Nocent, "La liturgie, activité et contemplation d'un peuple sacerdotal," in: *Notitiae,* 16 (1980) 178.

20. J. Jungmann, *The Place of Christ in Liturgical Prayer,* London, Geoffrey Chapman, 1965, 144–171; A. Verheul, *Introduction to the Liturgy,* 21–72.

21. Praefatio Paschalis III: "Qui se pro nobis offérre non desinit, nosque apud te perénni advocatione defendit; qui immolatus iam non moritur, sed semper vivit occisus," echoing Heb. 7:25, Rom. 6:9, Rev. 1:8, *Missale Romanum,* 407.

22. Dominica IV Adventus, Super oblata: "Altari tuo, superposita munera Spiritus ille sanctificet, qui beatae Mariae viscera sua virtute replevit"; Prex Eucharistica II: "Haec ergo dona, quaesumus, Spiritus tui rore sanctifica, ut nobis Corpus et Sanguis fiant Domini nostri Iesu Christi"; Prex Eucharistica III: "Supplices ergo te, Domine, deprecamur, ut haec munera, quae tibi sacranda detulimus, eodem Spiritu sanctificare digneris, ut Corpus et Sanguis fiant Filii tui Domini nostri Iesu Christi"; Prex Eucharistica IV: "Quaesumus igitur, Domine, ut idem Spiritus Sanctus haec munera sanctificare dignetur, ut Corpus et Sanguis fiant Domini nostri Iesu Christi," *Missale Romanum,* 132, 457, 461, 468 respectively. B. Botte, *La Tradition Apostolique de Saint Hippolyte, Essai de reconstitution,* Oratio consecrationis episcopi: "nunc effunde eam virtutem, quae a te est, principalis sp(iritu)s, quem dedisti dilecto filio tuo Ie(s)u Chr(ist)o, quod donauit sanctis apostolis, qui constituerunt ecclesiam," 8.

23. Jn. 4:23–24: "But the hour is coming, and now is, when the true worshipers will worship the Father in spirit and truth, for such the Father seeks to worship him. God is spirit, and those who worship him must worship in spirit and truth."

24. Rom. 8:15b–16: "When we cry, "Abba! Father!" it is the Spirit

himself bearing witness with our spirit that we are children of God";
26–27: "Likewise the Spirit helps us in our weakness; for we do not
know how to pray as we ought, but the Spirit himself intercedes for
us with sighs too deep for words. And he who searches the hearts of
men knows what is the mind of the Spirit, because the Spirit intercedes for the saints according to the will of God."

25. A. Verheul, *Introduction to the Liturgy,* 149–172; C. Stuhl-
müller, "Scriptural-Liturgical Depth in Christian Living" in: F.
McManus (ed.), *The Revival of the Liturgy,* New York, Herder and
Herder, 1963, 15–32; P. M. Guillaume, "The Reason for an Old Testament Lesson," in: L. Sheppard (ed.), *The New Liturgy,* London, Darton, Longman and Todd, 1970, 59–72.

26. *Dei Verbum* 23.

27. A. Nocent, *Le Messe avant et après Saint Pie V,* Paris, Éditions Beauchesne, 1977, "On sait comment le chant prendra un tel
développement que les lectures tendront à diminuer de longueur
pour leur faire place; le secondaire parvient ainsi à supplanter l'es-
sentiel et la celébration de la parole mérite de moins en moins son
nom. Il en sera surtout ainsi au moment où, et ce faut assez tôt pour
certaines régions, la langue latine ne fut plus comprise": 28–29.

28. J. Jungmann, *The Mass of the Roman Rite,* 168–176. Participation through the exercise of liturgical lay ministries is in the process of development in many countries; pastoral needs and theological
reflection will determine its evolution: C. Marivoet, "Lay Ministries
in the Philippines," in: *The Liturgical Information Bulletin of the
Philippines,* 9 (1976) 56–85.

29. A. Nocent, *La Messe avant et après Saint Pie V:* "Ce serait
vers le temps de saint Léon-le-Grand (440–461), que serait apparue
l'oraison du début, à l'époque ou la creativité prend dans la liturgie
de Rome une place importante": 28.

30. Ignatius to the Philadelphians, IV, 1; Ignatius to the Smyrneans, VIII, 1, in: P. Camelot (ed.), *Sources Chrétiennes,* 10 (1945)
110–111, 126–129.

31. N. M. Denis-Boulet-R. Beraudy, "The Eucharist," in: A. G.
Martimort (ed.), *The Church at Prayer,* Shannon, Irish University
Press, 1973, 172.

32. D. Power, "Sacramental Celebration and Liturgical Ministry," in: *Concilium,* February 1972, 26–42; P. Tena, "The Liturgical
Assembly and Its President," *ibid.,* 43–54.

33. C. Vagaggini, *Il senso teologico della liturgia,* 46–106; A. G.

Martimort, "Sacred Signs," in: *The Church at Prayer,* 146–179; A. Vergote, "Symbolic Gestures and Actions in the Liturgy," in: *Concilium,* February 1971, 40–52.

31. J. Jungmann, *The Mass: An Historical, Theological, and Pastoral Survey,* Collegeville, The Liturgical Press, 1976, 208. Cf., A. Nocent, *The Future of the Liturgy,* New York, Herder and Herder, 1963, 174–176.

35. J. Jeremias, *The Eucharistic Words of Jesus,* London, SCM, 1966, 224.

36. J.-M. Van Cangh, *La multiplication des pains et l'eucharistie,* Paris, Les Editions du Cerf, 1975, 67–109.

37. "Mais il faut s'efforcer aussi de communiquer fidèlement à un peuple donné et dans son propre langage ce que l'Eglise a voulu communiquer par le texte original à un autre peuple et dans une autre langue. La fidélité d'une traduction ne peut donc être jugée seulement à partir de chaque phrase, mais elle doit l'être d'après le contexte exact de la communication liturgique en conformité avec sa nature et ses modes propres": *Instructions officielles sur les nouveaux rites de la messe, le calendier, les traductions liturgiques,* Paris, 1969, 192. Cf. as well its last article cited in footnote 14 of Chapter III. A. Triacca, "Creatività eucologica: motivazioni per una sua giustificazione teorica e linee pratiche metodologiche," in: *Ephemerides Liturgicae,* 89 (1975) 100–118; A. Rousseau, "Discussion sur les limites d'une analyse du vocabulaire liturgique," in: *La Maison-Dieu,* 25 (1976) 85–96.

38. S. Marsili, "Liturgical Texts for Modern Man," in: *Concilium,* 42 (1969) 49–70.

39. G. Venturi, "Evoluzione della problematica relativa alla traduzione liturgica," in: *Mysterion, Miscellanea liturgica in occasione dei 70 anni dell'Abate Salvatore Marsili,* Torino, Elle di ci editrice, 1981, 324–327.

40. D. Saliers, "On the 'Crisis' of Liturgical Language," in: *Worship,* 44 (1970) 399–411.

41. Pauli VI, "Allocutio ad interpretes" die 10 novembris 1965: "Etsi sermo vulgaris, cui nunc locus est in Sacra Liturgia, omnium, etiam parvulorum et rudium, captui debet esse accommodatus, semper tamen, ut probe nostris, dignus sit oportet rebus celsissimis, quae eo significantur, diversus a cotidiana loquendi consuetudine, quae in viis et foris viget, talis, ut animi sensus tangat et corda Dei amore inflammet"; *Acta Apostolicae Sedis,* 57 (1965) 968.

Chapter Five

1. B. Neunheuser, "The 'Sacramentarium Gelasianum' (Reg. lat. 316) and Its Significance in Liturgical History," in: *Sacramentarium Gelasianum e codice Vaticano Reginensi latino 316 vertente anno sacro MCMLXXV iussu Pauli Pp. VI phototypice editum,* in civitate Vaticana, 1975, I; "... when pilgrims came in ever greater numbers to Rome from the north, from the young churches of Gaul ... (they) looked on in wonderment at the liturgy in the shrines and basilicas of the city. Then they took back with them what they could acquire: manuscript copies, first of single *libelli,* then of whole sacramentaries. At home they used these texts freely adapting them to their own needs and local conditions": 34.

2. R. Beals *et al., An Introduction to Anthropology,* London, Collier Macmillan Publishers, 1977 (fifth edition), 25–28, 704.

3. X. Seumois, "Norme per adattare la liturgia al carattere ed alla tradizioni del diversi popoli," in: V. Joannes (ed.), *op. cit.,* 78–79.

4. F. Jocano, *Growing Up in a Philippine Barrio,* New York, Holt, Rinehart and Winston, 1969; Lynch-Frank-Guzman (ed.), *Four Readings on Philippine Values,* Quezon City, Ateneo de Manila Press, 1970; H. De La Costa, "The Filipino National Tradition," in: R. Bonoan (ed.), *Challenge for the Filipino,* Quezon City, Ateneo Publications Office, 1971, 42–56; OCR, PA, *Towards the Restructuring of Filipino Values,* 1973.

5. L. Concepcion, "Architecture in the Philippines," in: *National Museum Lectures,* Manila, October 1967 (second of a series); A. Molina, "Music in the Philippines," in *ibid.,* November 1967 (third of a series); G. Ocampo, "Contemporary Painting of the Philippines," in *ibid.,* February 1968 (seventh of a series); cf. also A. Coseteng, *Spanish Churches in the Philippines,* Quezon City, New Mercury Printing Press, 1972.

6. G. Guthrie, *The Psychology of Modernization in the Rural Philippines,* Quezon City, Ateneo de Manila University Press, 1971.

7. Y. Raguin, "Indigenization of the Church," in: *Teaching All Nations,* 6 (1969) 154.

8. D. Amalorpavadass, *Towards Indigenization in the Liturgy,* 55.

9. Y. Raguin, *op. cit.,* 160–164.

10. J. G. Frazer, *op. cit.,* 930–934.

11. A. Chupungco, "A Filipino Attempt at Liturgical Indigenization," in: *Ephemerides Liturgicae,* 91 (1977) 371–372.

12. A. Rowbotham, *op. cit.,* 128–129.

13. V. Gorospe, *Christian Renewal of Filipino Values,* Quezon City, Ateneo de Manila University Press, 1966, 19–59.

14. B. Gantin, "Evangelization in Africa Today: Development of the Local Indigenous Church and Collaboration of Foreign Missionaries," in: *Omnis Terra,* 73 (Jan. 1976) 99–110.

15. C. Kraft, *Christianity in Culture,* New York, Orbis Books, 1979, 64–80.

16. E. Bishop, *Liturgica Historica,* Oxford, Clarendon Press, 1918, 12.

17. SC 6–7.

18. A. Chupungco, "A Historical Survey of Liturgical Adaptation," in: *Notitiae,* 17 (1981) 29–31.

19. *Instructions officielles sur les nouveaux rites de la messe, le calendier, les traductions liturgiques,* Paris, 1969, 191–192.

20. T. Klauser, *A Short History of the Western Liturgy,* Oxford, Oxford University Press, 1979 (second edition), 109–113.

21. Cf., for instance, L. C. Mohlberg (ed.), *Missale Gothicum,* Rome, Casa Editrice Herder, 1961, 25.

22. B. Neunheuser, *Storia della liturgia attraverso le epoche culturali,* Roma, Edizioni liturgiche, 1977, 117–120.

23. *Instructions officielles . . . ,* 203–204.

24. L. C. Mohlberg, (ed.), *Sacramentarium Veronense,* Roma, Herder Editrice e Libreria, 1978, 157.

25. This translation is inspired by the English rendition of the second preface for weekdays.

26. LG 13, AG 22.

27. J. P. Audet, *Didaché,* Paris, J. Gabalda, 1958, 232.

28. W. E. Oesterley, *The Jewish Background of Christian Liturgy,* Oxford, Clarendon Press, 1925, 111–155.

29. *Ordo Celebrandi Matrimonium,* Typis Polyglottis Vaticanis, 1972, "Praenotanda," 13–16, 9–10.

30. *Ibid.,* "Praenotanda," 17–18, 10.

31. A. P. Ratu, *An Adoption of the Adat Marriage Rites of the Dawanese People of Timor, Indonesia, as a Proposed Marriage Rite for Dawanese Catholics,* Manila, East Asian Pastoral Institute, 1973; A. Chupungco (ed.), *Liturgical Renewal in the Philippines,* "Benguet Marriage Rite—Towards A Liturgical Indigenization" (14–26), "Bontoc Marriage Rite—A Study on Liturgical Indigenization" (27–44), "Kalinga Marriage Rite—A Study on Liturgical Indigenization" (45–70).

32. Mansi (ed.), *Sacrorum Conciliorum nova et amplissima collec-*

tio, Parisiis, Expensis Huberti Welter, Bibliopolae, 1892, 33 "Concilii Tridentini Decretum de Reformatione Matrimonii "Tametsi," I, 153.

33. SC 77.

34. *Ordo Celebrandi Matrimonium,* "Praenotanda," 1, 7.

35. B. Botte, "Le probleme de l'adaptation en liturgie," in: *Revue du Clergé Africain,* 18 (1963) 303–319.

Conclusion

1. *Notitiae* 14 (1978), n. 139, p. 74.

Suggested Reading

Baumstark, A., *Comparative Liturgy* (Revised by B. Botte), Translation by F. L. Cross, The Newman Press, Westminister, Maryland, 1958.

Bishop, E., *Liturgica Historica: Papers on the Liturgy and Religious Life of the Western Church,* The Clarendon Press, Oxford, 1918.

Chupungco, A., "A Filipino Attempt at Liturgical Indigenization," *Ephemerides Liturgicae,* Vol. 91 (1977), pp. 370–376.

———"The Magna Carta of Liturgical Adaptation," *Notitiae,* Vol. 14 (1978), pp. 75–89.

———"A Filipino Adaptation of the Liturgical Language," *Eulogia Miscellanea Liturgica in Onore di P. Burkhard Neunheuser, O. S. B.,* Analecta Liturgica 1. Editrice Anselmiana, Rome, 1979, pp. 45–55.

———"Greco-Roman Culture and Liturgical Adaptation," *Notitiae,* Vol. 15 (1979), pp. 202–218.

———"A Historical Survey of Liturgical Adaptation," *Notitiae,* Vol. 17 (1981), pp. 28–43.

Collins, M., "Liturgical Methodology and the Cultural Evolution of Worship in the United States," *Worship,* Vol. 49 (1975), pp. 85–102.

Crichton, J. D., *Changes in the Liturgy,* Alba House, Staten Island, New York, 1965.

Diekmann, G., "Is There a Distinct American Contribution to the Liturgical Renewal?" *Worship,* Vol. 45 (1971), pp. 578–587.

Eisenhofer, L. and Lechner, J., *The Liturgy of the Roman Rite* (Edited by H. E. Winstone), Translation by A. J. and E. F. Peeler, Herder and Herder, New York, 1960.

Escamilla, R., "Worship in the Context of the Hispanic Culture," *Worship,* Vol. 51 (1977), pp. 290–293.

Gusmer, C., "A Bill of Rites: Liturgical Adaptation in America," *Worship,* Vol. 51 (1977), pp. 283–289.

Hahn, F., *The Worship of the Early Church,* Translation by J. Reumann, Fortress Press, Philadelphia, 1973.

Jungmann, J., *The Mass of the Roman Rite,* 2 vols., Translation by F. A. Brunner, Benziger Brothers, Inc., New York, 1951–1955.

——*The Early Liturgy to the Time of Gregory the Great,* Translation by F. A. Brunner. University of Notre Dame Press, Notre Dame, Indiana, 1959.

——*Pastoral Liturgy,* Translation by Challoner Publications, Herder and Herder, New York, 1962.

——*The Place of Christ in Liturgical Prayer,* Translation by A. Peeler, Alba House, Staten Island, New York, 1965.

——"Constitution on the Sacred Liturgy," *Commentary on the Documents of Vatican II,* Vol. 1 (Edited by H. Vorgrimler), Translation by L. Adolphus, Herder and Herder, New York, 1967, pp. 1–87.

King, A., *Notes on the Catholic Liturgies,* Longmans, Green, and Company, London, 1930.

——*Liturgies of the Religious Orders,* Longmans, Green, and Company, 1955.

——*Liturgies of the Primatial Sees,* Longmans, Green, and Company, 1957.

——*Liturgy of the Roman Church,* Bruce Publishing Company, Milwaukee, Wisconsin, 1957.

——*Liturgies of the Past,* Bruce Publishing Company, Milwaukee, Wisconsin, 1959.

Mahoney, F., "The Aymara Indians: A Model for Liturgical Adaptation," *Worship,* Vol. 45 (1971), pp. 405–413.

National Office for Black Catholics and The Liturgical Conference, Editors, *This Far by Faith: American Black Worship and Its African Roots,* The Liturgical Conference, Washington, D.C., 1977.

Power, D., "Cult to Culture: The Liturgical Foundation of Theology," *Worship,* Vol. 54 (1980), pp. 482–495.

Puthanangady, P., "Liturgical Renewal in India," *Ephemerides Liturgicae,* Vol. 91 (1977), pp. 350–366.

Ramírez, R., "Liturgy from the Mexican American Perspective," *Worship,* Vol. 51 (1977), pp. 293–298.

Shaughnessy, J., Editor, *The Roots of Ritual,* Wm. B. Eerdmans, Grand Rapids, Michigan, 1973.

Smits, K., "Liturgical Reform in Cultural Perspective," *Worship,* Vol. 50 (1976), pp. 98–110.

Turner, V., *The Ritual Process,* Aldine Publishing Company, Chicago, 1969.

Van Dijk, S.J.P. and Walker, J.H., *The Origins of the Modern Roman Liturgy,* The Newman Press, Westminster, Maryland, 1960.

Van Dijk, S.J.P., *Sources of the Modern Roman Liturgy,* 2 vols., E. J. Brill, Leiden, 1963.

Werner, E., *The Sacred Bridge: Liturgical Parallels in Synagogue and Early Church,* Schocken Books, Inc., New York, 1970.

White, J. *Christian Worship in Transition,* Abingdon, Nashville, Tennessee, 1976.

Willis, G., *Essays in Early Roman Liturgy,* Alcuin Club Series No. 46, S.P.C.K., London, 1964.

——*Further Essays in Early Roman Liturgy,* Alcuin Club Series No. 50, S.P.C.K., London, 1968.

9937